C000006490

A Mother's
LOVE

Murder took Bridie McGoldrick's
child; forgiving his killer
changed everything.

LORNA FARRELL

I hope this book Blesses
you ~ God is Faithful

McKnight
& Bishop
Ltd

lorna farrell.

About The Publisher

McKnight & Bishop are always on the lookout for new authors and ideas for new books. If you write or if you have an idea for a book, please email:

info@mcknightbishop.com

Some things we love are undiscovered authors, open-source software, Creative Commons, crowd-funding, Amazon/Kindle, faith, social networking, laughter and new ideas.

Visit us at **www.mcknightbishop.com**

Copyright © Lorna Farrell 2020

The rights of Lorna Farrell to be identified as the Author of this Work has been asserted by her in accordance with Section 77 of the Copyright, Designs and Patents Act 1988.

ISBN 978-1-905691-70-8

A CIP catalogue record for this book is available from the British Library.

First published in 2021 by McKnight & Bishop Inspire, an imprint of:

McKnight & Bishop Ltd
26 Walworth Crescent, Darlington DL3 0TX
http://www.mcknightbishop.com | info@mcknightbishop.com

This book has been typeset in Garamond, Century Gothic and
COPPERPLATE GOTHIC BOLD

Cover Photo of Lorna Farrell by Graeme Hewitson at monument**photos**

Printed and bound in Great Britain by United Print, 16 Great Queen Street, London WC2B 5AH

I want to dedicate this book to my two boys,
Martin and Matthew, you are the greatest achievement
in my life and I am so proud and blessed to be your mum.
I love you both forever and I am so proud of who you are
and how well you do life; you are the VERY best of me.
Thanks for letting me drive the taxi!!

Contents

Acknowledgements

Although it has been a passion and a privilege to write this book, I could not have done it without the help and support of several people, especially the incomparable Bridie McGoldrick.

Firstly, I would like to thank all my friends and family who enrich my life whether I am writing a book or not. I love and appreciate you. You all make the story of my life so much better, funnier, safer and more colourful.

To Jamie Kimmett who has encouraged me, believed in me, created a website for me, read and reread extracts and Prayed frequently for this book. Love you pal and I appreciate your support.

To my daughter-in-love Shannon and grandson Liam; I love you. Thank you for brightening up my life, encouraging me, and unlocking a depth of love as a gran that I never knew was possible.

My mum, Lottie; I love you. Thank you for a lifetime of looking for the best in people, laughs and the best chocolate cake ever!

Elaine, Lewis and Melanie; I love you lots and I'm so glad you're in my life; here's to plenty more giggles and bad accents

To Shirley and Skye; I love you and wish Gods best for you.

To Shona Leishman, Nicola Leonard, Lindsey Danvers, Kirsteen Gray, Kirsty Bell, Christine Cassie and Heather Malloy; thank you for years of love, hugs, laughs, prayers, tears, encouragement and treacle scones. You are amazing, wonderful women.

To Graeme Mathie; your support and timely encouragement are massively appreciated. Thanks for being so faithful.

Heartfelt thanks to my amazing prayer warriors and life group friends: Lorna and Jim Whitelaw, Neil and Dawn Ingall, Graeme and Dorothy Templeton, Jenny Wilson and Irene Clydesdale. You are such faithful blessings.

Thanks also to wise and godly teachers who help to keep my eyes and heart focused on Jesus; who have given me such a love for the Word of God as I have tried to write this book to honour him. Thanks to Revd Scott Kirkland, Kenneth Ross, Bart Gavigan, Mark Cairney, Ruari O'Brien, David Graham and Dr Bob Fyall.

A big shout out to my girls at Queens Park Women's Football Club; you are all legends. And to George Watson and everyone involved in the beautiful game at Queens Park FC; thank you for the privilege of being your chaplain and loudest fan!

Massive heartfelt thanks to Mark Fleming and all at Sports Chaplaincy UK. It's such a Blessing to be part of this awesome ministry.

Thanks also to those who have literally made this book happen, whom I all consider to be friends.

To my editor, Joy; I am eternally indebted to you. Thanks for taking my heartfelt but untidy ramblings and making them coherent and effective. You are a gentle, encouraging, brilliant editor and you wield that red ink with love and compassion. Thank you for making this story a book, and for becoming such a blessing and a friend in the process.

To publishing genius and graphic designer, Mark McKnight; thank you for your patience, excellence and amazing versatility. I love that you understood my vision and were so easy to work with (and sorry it took quite so long!).

To Jacqueline McGoldrick, Martin McGoldrick, Tom Lennon and Christina Devine, who gave so generously of their time to share some of their memories and love for Bridie with me.

To Joe Forker, who drove me all around Northern Ireland and captivated me with his stories, his faith, his fun and his support for Bridie.

To anyone who buys this book- Thank you and I hope you are as amazed by Bridie's story and Faith as I have been.

Finally, I want to thank God himself for orchestrating my meeting with and enabling me to befriend the remarkable Bridie McGoldrick, and for his faithful love through Jesus Christ and the guidance he gives through his Holy Spirit. Thank you, Lord, for being the wings both Bridie and I shelter beneath.

Psalm 91:4 (NIV):
"He will cover you with his feathers, and under his wings you will find refuge; his faithfulness will be your shield and rampart."

Chapter 1:
I Belong To Glasgow

When they placed Michael in her arms, Bridie McGoldrick was flooded with pure and unconditional love. With a husband she adored and a son she had dearly longed for, her life was complete and she knew this love would last forever.

Despite having been a resident of Northern Ireland for most of her adult life, Bridie's story begins in an area on the south side of Glasgow known as 'the Gorbals'. For some, the mere mention of this area evokes images of gang warfare, impoverished kids and washing lines hanging across the street, but nothing could have been further from the truth for young Bridie McGeown, whose home was a warm, loving place filled with laughter.

Bridie was born on March 2, 1943. The third child of Irish Catholic parents John and Christine, who was known as Teeny. Bridie was the quietest of the seven kids, which may come as a surprise to those who know her today. Despite this, she was always at the heart of whatever was happening in their busy home.

The eldest McGeown child was John, followed by Joe, Bridie, Patrick, twin sisters Margaret and Mary Theresa (Margaret survived, but Mary Theresa tragically died from diphtheria at just two months old) and Frank. John had been married before he met Christine, but his first wife had sadly died. As a result, Bridie had an older half-brother called Bernard, whom she only met once when she was a little girl, as he was killed in action in Africa. She vividly remembers her girlish delight at the meeting, as Bernard bought her loads of her favourite 'scraps': glossy pictures shaped like angels, cherubs, fairies and the like, which children collected and kept in large scrapbooks.

Like so many families growing up in this era, sacrifices had to be made in the McGeown household so the kids didn't go without, but Bridie barely noticed, simply enjoying a carefree childhood. They had warm fires in all the rooms and food on the table each mealtime. There was laughter every single day, and she enjoyed being part of a close-knit family that made her feel wonderfully safe and secure. Bridie was also aware that her parents had distinct roles. Her father was the head of the household, while her mother ran everything within it like clockwork.

One room in particular was the 'engine room' of the household for working-class homes in Glasgow during the forties and fifties. The kitchen was where the McGeowns ate their meals, chatted and played games. Like the perfect advert for Scottish fare, the family would sit happily before great bowls of piping-hot porridge every winter's day. It was plain food by today's standards but, indicative of the era, it was simple, hearty and wholesome! The kitchen was also the place where the family would come together to pray; something that hugely influenced the young Bridie.

There may have been little spare cash in their childhood home, but there were plenty of high standards. The McGeowns were brought up to be polite, always saying their pleases and thank yous, and everyone knew to eat everything on their plates, whether they liked it or not. There was only one thing young Bridie would never eat: carrots. Even today the taste and texture make her shudder. Back in the day she could rely on Pat and John to eat them off her plate, as both boys loved them. The McGeown household always had napkins on the table. These were made up of old sheets or scraps of linen and came in all shapes and sizes, but the table was always set with them, and they sat together as a family to eat all their meals.

The family's special Sabbath routine became extremely important to Bridie. They all went to chapel together in their best clothes and with their brightest smiles. The children were under strict instructions from their father to face the front and never to turn around or misbehave. But although John was a stickler for discipline he was a kind man, and the children all knew they were loved and wanted. Even back then, Bridie knew this was a blessing not all of her friends enjoyed. Some Saturday nights John would wrap cloths or pipe cleaners around the girls' wet hair to make it curly the next day. He loved being hands-on with the kids, and Bridie adored her strong yet gentle daddy.

Bridie's father called her Bounty after the song "Bye, Baby Bunting" because she was such a hardworking, caring little girl who always tried her best to please her parents and mind her manners. But there was another reason for the nickname John used for his eldest daughter: the fact she was so generous with her time and belongings. Although she liked gifts as much as anyone else, Bridie never asked for anything and often gave things away to folks who had less than she did. John described her as a 'bountiful' child and said he would happily have had another seven of her.

It came as a great surprise to Bridie when she realised that her parents had Christian names and weren't just called "Mummy" and "Daddy", as that was how the pair addressed each other at home. This was typical among close-knit families, so it hadn't occurred to the young girl that her parents also had names!

Bridie's happy childhood provided the perfect springboard for her own family and church life later on. The rough and tumble, tears and cheers of coming from a large family, with all its noise and nurture, equipped her well for a life of love in the family of God. She easily accepted that giving was an important part of living, and she was particularly impacted by Jesus' words in Matthew 25:40 that "whatever you did for one of the least of these brothers and sisters of mine, you did for me". Her faith is the cornerstone of her life to this day, and she shares it easily with others.

Young Bridie's Catholic faith also had an important influence on her wardrobe. She was delighted that they all had chapel clothes, Sunday play clothes, everyday clothes and school clothes to wear. She also loved all the accessories: the straw bonnets for Easter, the shiny black patent-leather shoes she could see her face in, and the beautiful ribbons for her hair. Bridie particularly loved a beautiful red belted coat she had, which was lined with soft fur, and the young fashionista felt like the bee's knees every time she put it on. She always changed out of her best clothes to play with her siblings and friends, however.

The whole family was treated to an annual Eglington Street trip on the south side of Glasgow for sou'westers and rain macs, something that delighted the young girl with a keen eye for fun and fashion. There were bright yellow jackets for the girls and black for the boys, and once they had them in their clutches they couldn't wait to get outside to play in the rain and puddles. The west coast of Scotland offered plenty of opportunity for that!

Being one of two girls had its disadvantages, however. One year Bridie found her beloved sou'wester in bright red. She couldn't wait to dazzle while she splashed in the puddles, but as the shop didn't have one in Margaret's size both girls ended up with the familiar yellow one. Bridie considered this to be all Margaret's fault and a terrible travesty in terms of her own style aspirations.

An important part of the girls' wardrobe was their national dress: the kilt. Bridie wore the Black Watch tartan, which she adored. Every night they would return home from school and change into it. She loved the way the fabric moved and hung on her. Christine used to joke that Bridie had a great backside for a kilt! Bridie still loves shopping for outfits and always manages to find a bargain; her upbringing having instilled in her a love for thriftiness as well as style.

Bridie's mother Christine was also a strong character. She kept her little brood clean and safe, and gave them wholesome values to hold on to. As a little girl Bridie yearned to imitate her mum, and she watched with fascination as Christine navigated family life. The rooms were kept spick and span and Christine was always washing or baking. The children also had chores to do, and they were encouraged to have fun while they helped with the cleaning and polishing, but they would be in big trouble if they ever misbehaved!

Christine was also determined to show Bridie that her security could be found within the four walls of their home. Christine created an atmosphere of great happiness, and despite any financial difficulties they faced she never let the kids go without. While ensuring that each child had the new clothes and shoes they needed for every occasion, Christine made do with the same dress, coat and shoes for years. Despite this, Bridie recalls her mother always appearing smart and elegant. She had the softest skin and looked much younger than her years. She worked hard, but there was always singing, laughter and fun to be had. Theirs was a noisy household full of animated conversation and practical jokes, but there was also plenty of space to be themselves.

Even during her early years Bridie was a sensitive soul, and she would cry if the boys were ever smacked. On these occasions Christine would slap her across the legs and say, "There you are, young madam. That'll give you something to cry for." That might seem cruel by today's standards, but it was the norm back then. It didn't make Bridie feel abused or unloved; she knew her mother was just trying to keep them all in line.

While looking their best was expected in chapel, so was being on their best behaviour. Kids up and down the country were under no illusion as to the penalties of giving the family a 'showing up' in front of the congregation. Keeping a straight face and silently facing the front was particularly difficult one Sunday morning, however, as they sat waiting for Mass to start. Christine leaned forward to grab Frank, who had jumped off her knee, and accidentally passed wind very loudly. Quick as a flash, she scolded wee Frank at the top of her voice, feigning disgust that he had been so rude.

The whole family and everyone around them was laughing, as they all knew that no child could have made such a loud noise. Bridie recalls all the siblings being doubled up with laughter in their bedrooms when they got home, though they would never have dared laugh in Christine's face. Bridie McGoldrick continues to be a smart, co-ordinated and elegant dresser, and she has her warm Glasgow upbringing to thank for that. She may not be afraid to turn around in chapel these days, but Bridie always keeps her hair and make-up looking nice.

Not the sort of child known for disobeying her parents, Bridie remembers how a simple misunderstanding brought about an angry response from her father on one occasion when she used the phrase "Blast it!" The exclamation earned her a stinging slap from John, which left an angry red mark on her face. Horrified, she explained that she hadn't said the swear word he obviously thought she had. He replied that if he thought she had sworn, others might have made the same mistake. When she pointed out that she was a married woman by this point, he promptly informed her that it didn't give her the right to a dirty tongue!

Growing up, Bridie shared a bed with Margaret, who often wet herself in the night. Bridie was tired of waking up soaked but needed a creative mind to avoid hurting her younger sister's feelings, so she piled the covers up to make some space between them. Margaret was upset by this barrier and asked why they needed it. Bridie explained that every night when they fell asleep fairies came into their room and hopped up onto the covers between them. A very trusting Margaret fell asleep excitedly every night, dreaming of the magical little creatures dancing on the barrier! However, despite going to sleep happier, she still managed to pee on them both. Bridie enjoyed her role as big sister to Margaret, and these innocent, happy days of childhood set firm foundations that helped both women navigate harrowing circumstances in later life.

Life as a youngster was a lot of fun, coming as she did from a family of practical jokers... especially the boys! One night as Margaret and Bridie lay in bed, waiting on the fairies, the bed began to shake. It moved vigorously back and forth, terrifying the young sisters. The movement got faster and faster until the bed was shaking up and down and the pair were screaming loudly for their parents, convinced some hideous monster was about to attack them. Just as John and Christine ran into the room, their big brother Joe rolled out from under the bed, laughing hysterically and absolutely delighted with his successful trick.

Another night, two of the boys terrified their sisters with an illuminated skeleton on a pully. They waited until Bridie and Margaret were in bed, then made it move towards them in the dark. The sisters were absolutely terrified, and their screams must have reached as far as Gorbals Cross. John and Christine were firm with the boys, but Bridie could tell they were trying hard to keep their laughter inside on both occasions.

There was an emerging subculture of knives and gangs in Glasgow at this time, as many men struggled with unemployment. Bridie's family may not have been rich, but they were never truly poor, and John was a wonderful role model. Although they lived in an area that was rife with problems, it never seemed to impact their street or immediate neighbours, and the McGeown home was certainly untouched by violence and alcoholism. Bridie always knew John would tell her the truth, even if she didn't want to hear it!

Saturday nights when the pubs closed were interesting times for the McGeown family, as the live 'entertainment' enthralled and frustrated in equal measures. As Bridie and Margaret's bedroom window looked out onto the street below, John and Christine would come into the girls' room and sit beside the window in the dark, laughing as they listened to the drunks fighting or singing. The girls would lie in their beds, begging to be allowed up to see who was saying or doing what, but were usually told to "Ssshh!" and go to sleep. On a few occasions the boys were allowed in to watch, and the whole family would huddle together, stifling fits of giggles as the neighbours' drunken antics kept them amused for hours.

If they ever had a tiff, John and Christine would use the children to communicate with one another. Christine would say, "Bridie, ask your father to pass the salt, please." Or John would say, "Margaret, tell your mother I'll be back later tomorrow as I have a meeting after work." Bridie hated it when they had a fallout, rare as it was, but she always found this hilarious.

Bridie's nose was invariably stuck in a book, including her beloved Rupert Bear series. She read her favourite book continually and often used to drift away into Rupert's imaginary world until one of the others came rushing in to find her because she hadn't heard Christine shouting that it was chore time. The magical places and faraway lands in her books were a constant source of amazement to her as a young child, and Bridie could only dream of seeing some of the sights she had read about.

The McGeowns loved listening to the radio, and John fixed up receivers in all the rooms so they could tune in every night to listen to The Lone Ranger and hear songs by Roy Rogers. The whole family also loved quiz shows, with their memorable catchphrases and theme tunes. It thrilled Bridie to think that as she sat with her family listening to the shows, her friends up and down the neighbourhood were doing the same thing.

These childhood memories evoke a much-missed age of innocence for Bridie, when every household was part of the community; when people knew each other well and looked out for one another. Anyone who was disrespectful to the women or children would be swiftly dealt with via a few stern words from the other men, while any woman in need found a street full of ready-made counsellors waiting on her doorstep.

Bridie's childhood was a happy one, but it wasn't without tears. Two lively girls sharing a bed led to a high level of giggles, squeals, cries and squabbles. A certain amount of light slapping of little legs was also considered necessary by their parents. Always resourceful, Margaret thought she could outwit them and came up with the bright idea of rolling the sheets up over their legs and feet – hidden by the covers – to protect them. This might have worked well when Bridie and Margaret were being chastised had they not, instead of displaying the normal tears, been laughing out loud! Their wise mother knew something wasn't right. They were soon found out and their ingenious protection removed.

While some bear emotional scars from childhood, Bridie only has a few physical ones from the scrapes she got into. Recognising that the word of the comparatively quieter, better-behaved Bunty was always believed by their parents, Joe decided she would be the perfect person to climb up and grab the tinned jam their mother had tucked away on a high shelf. Hoisted up on his shoulders, a trembling Bridie grabbed the open tin just as Joe wobbled. She came crashing down, her finger cut by the jagged tin as she fell. Instead of jam, Bridie's finger was covered in blood. When the sock Joe put over it failed to stop the blood flowing, Bridie had to confess to her surprised mother that she was the culprit. She was known as 'the jam stealer' for a long time afterwards!

Margaret may have been the youngest girl and smallest child, but she was no lightweight, often ruling with a rod of iron. Bridie describes her as "the wee runt who was always the boss". The kids often played at schools, and Margaret always had to be the teacher. She used to make them all hold their hands out for the strap, which was one of their daddy's old belts, and she would slap her siblings with it, repeatedly and hard. It hurt like blazes, yet Bridie and her brothers put their hands out every time she insisted, falling for it every time.

Aside from red hands and injured pride, Bridie recalls the timely interruptions from their parents on more than one occasion when Margaret was in full flow. A game of dentists nearly ended in real tears once when Margaret examined their teeth and decided they all needed to come out. Thankfully, John came in just in time to stop her taking Frank's teeth out with a pair of pliers!

Another event in the home that still brings a smile to Bridie's face is Christmas. The McGeowns never missed out on a thing, and Bridie still recalls the magical excitement that enveloped the home at this time of year. She fondly remembers all the preparations leading up to it: making paper-chain decorations, hanging up their stockings on Christmas Eve, the brightly coloured tree that stood in the middle of the bedroom she and Margaret shared, the balloons and crepe paper they hung on it, and even the rug that spread across the floor so nobody's feet were cold on Christmas morning. She was enthralled by the way the embers of the fire sparkled against the tree, transforming the whole place into a magical wonderland.

The whole family would get up bright and early on Christmas morning and head into the kitchen, where the table would be piled high with presents. They would each receive an orange, a silver thruppenny bit (a three-pence coin), a nightgown, a new school satchel, a pair of slippers and a bar of Highland toffee. One year Bridie was absolutely delighted to find a school case waiting for her rather than a satchel, and once again she thought it was the bee's knees. She couldn't wait to get back to school to show it off. Bridie and Margaret had such fun carrying pencils, jotters and colouring-in books inside them, and any other bits and bobs they could fit in there. To a bunch of kids living in the Gorbals during the fifties they were a real treasure; just locking and unlocking them was a source of fun for their little fingers. Their parents had scrimped and saved to ensure that each child would be happy with their gifts, and this particular present really stuck in Bridie's mind. After opening their gifts, the whole family would go to Mass before enjoying a Christmas dinner of homemade soup followed by boiled chicken, potatoes and vegetables, with an extra helping of carrots for Joe and Pat!

John and Christine taught the children to look out for each other and always stick together, which Margaret used to her advantage. She saw Bridie as a "wee goody two shoes" who never lied or broke the rules, and she used to tease her sister about it. But while Margaret was always getting herself into trouble, Bridie often had to help get her out of it.

The sisters became closer and closer as they learned to do life in a tough area amid unrelenting economic and social pressures. One particular year, everybody in the old Glasgow neighbourhood wanted bikes, and the streets were filled with children zipping around on them. Naturally, the McGeown children were hounding their parents, but unbeknown to them John and Christine had been saving up their money for weeks.

One evening John arrived home from work with three bikes, and the kids all gathered around excitedly. One was for John and Joe to share, another was for Margaret and Pat, and there was a tricycle for Frank. Bridie was gutted, as it seemed there was nothing for her, but she should have known her parents would never leave anyone out, and it wasn't long before Christine produced a pair of roller skates from behind her back.

Bridie was ecstatic, as she had wanted a pair for ages. She spent hours learning how to skate, leaning against her mum as she gingerly moved around the streets feeling so grown up. Those roller skates were her pride and joy, and she spent every waking minute on them. To her horror, she came home from school one day to discover they were missing. She looked everywhere but they were nowhere to be found. John and Joe were building something outside and swore they hadn't seen them. Bridie was inconsolable and imagined her mother would also be fuming given the money she had so carefully saved to buy them.

The culprits were soon revealed, however. John and Joe had been busy constructing the most Scottish of playthings: the 'bogie'. This type of vehicle, made from string, cardboard boxes and planks of wood atop a set of wheels would be raced through the streets with great pleasure. It turned out Bridie's roller skates had been used as the wheels for this quirky contraption! She was initially distraught, but, blessed with a level of diplomacy that always solved everything, Daddy declared it 'Bunty's Bogie' and the delighted Bridie took charge of her new toy. Meanwhile, John and Joe took charge of a few tears of regret!

Listening to her mother sing soprano on an old cassette one night, 13-year-old Bridie made the shock discovery that her parents were Irish! Weird as it sounds, it wasn't until she heard the lilt on the old recording that she twigged. Up until then they had just been Mummy and Daddy. She soon came to love her Irish heritage, which is still an integral part of her DNA. The country, the people, the patter and the local church are every bit as important as her Scottish roots. Bridie has always had a truly Celtic heart and soul.

The McGeowns travelled to Ireland every year, and Bridie enjoyed every minute. She felt sad to leave the land and people they loved at the end of each holiday, but she knew they would soon be back. The whole family felt a pull and an affinity to the country, but Northern Ireland would forever hold a special place in Little Miss Bunty's heart. Proud to be Scottish, the childhood dilemma she faced with regard to where 'home' was has long been settled for Bridie. Home was most definitely wherever the heart was, and for this fun-loving, faith-filled woman of hope that could only mean one thing: family. This made the tragedy that was to unfold a little later in her life even more horrific.

CHAPTER 2:
The Other Side Of The Glasgow Coin

It certainly wasn't all fun and games for the McGeowns, as the conditions in post-war Glasgow were harsh. Bridie saw depravation all around her as families struggled to enjoy even the most basic of necessities, with some of her friends living below the poverty line and experiencing serious lack. She noticed with sadness that some of the children couldn't concentrate at school because they were starving or always had colds due to the damp, cramped conditions at home. Diseases and infections spread like wildfire in large families that lived huddled together in just one or two rooms. The fact the McGeowns always had a warm home and food on the table made them far better off than many other families in their street. Too young to form any real social or political rationale, Bridie simply knew that some people had a much higher mountain to climb than others.

People were still using ration books at this time, but Christine had a knack of making their provisions last. The neighbours would often come to ask for a bit of sugar or butter, or perhaps an egg, and

Bridie noticed that her mother never asked for it back, something she appreciated and admired. There was one particular neighbour who had very little, and each week Christine would make a little parcel of tea, sugar, cheese, butter, bacon and sausage, all wrapped in newspaper, and send it round to her. Rations could only go so far, but Christine's generosity and community spirit went much further.

Even from a young age, Bridie noticed that not everyone appreciated the size of her close-knit family. Many of the wealthier women from other communities were disgusted by the number of kids the McGeowns had and made no effort to hide it. Bridie knew there were families living nearby that had more money and belongings than hers, but she was confident that no one had more joy than their happy brood.

Christine had to put up with a fair bit of backbiting and many scornful glances from these women, but she never let this bother her and it certainly had minimal impact on her kids, who were so close a bit of gossip didn't worry them too much. Bridie sometimes felt upset about the funny looks and whispers as she got older, but she knew without a doubt that her family was blessed to be so large and loving.

Although never embraced or even understood during Bridie's childhood, sectarianism continually reared its vicious head. Like so many other urban regions after the Second World War, the Gorbals area was overpopulated and lacked basic facilities. The south side of Glasgow was home to a large immigrant Irish population, and this added to the growing rivalry between the two main football clubs, Celtic and Rangers, collectively known as 'the Old Firm'. Celtic was predominantly supported by Catholics and Rangers by Protestants. Neighbours were often suspicious of those on 'the other side', and this caused bitter and often bloody disputes.

The Old Firm rivalry among children mainly consisted of singing songs, but Bridie received a harsh rebuke from her father once when she was called inside to explain why she was singing "Are you a Billy or a Dan or an old Tin can?" (Protestant, Catholic or Jew). This resulted in a swift slap across the back of her legs and she was told never to sing it again.

One common event across the country at this time was the 'moonlight flit', when whole families would up sticks in the middle of the night, taking their meagre belongings with them because they couldn't afford to pay the rent. Bridie remembers two of her friends disappearing this way. Some folks were so desperate they had to uproot their kids from school and settle somewhere new, miles away from their friends and families.

Years later at one of Glasgow's most famous institutions, the Barras – a long street in the East End of Glasgow with a giant indoor market, so called after the barrows the traders used to sell from – Bridie bumped into her friend Evelyn, who had been forced to 'do a flit' as a youngster. There was no sense of shame or embarrassment; those had been tough times, and for many families it was simply about survival. When Bridie thinks about her friend from childhood, she doesn't dwell on the flit. It was the beautiful, thick, bright blonde hair Evelyn had, which her mother used to plait and then tie with a bright yellow bow, that sticks in her mind. Even then, style mattered!

Many of the women in poorer Scottish communities were strong, resourceful matriarchs who ensured that life ran as smoothly as possible for their families. Bridie loved seeing the older girls and some of the married women drawing a brown line up their backs of their legs to look like they had seamed stockings on. It was a risky thing to do, given how much it rains in Glasgow!

The women of the Gorbals weren't averse to dishing out their own form of justice. At one time their southside community was being targeted by a flasher. He would come along on his bike and take young girls up the road under the pretence of showing them his bike, but when he got them there he would expose his privates. On one occasion he did this on Bridie's street and someone ran to tell their mother. A whole mob of irate tenement mothers came out to chase the guy, and they gave him a swift and severe beating on the street. Some women used rolling pins, while others brought their metal basins out, and one by one they administered justice. The police were then called and the perpetrator was taken away and charged.

Another common issue in this post-war community was the plight of soldiers who had returned from service and were 'shell-shocked'. Nowadays this would be classified as post-traumatic stress disorder, and counselling, therapy, medication and other resources might be offered, but this simply wasn't the case in the fifties and sixties. Bridie remembers the father of her friend Anna sitting in the corner of their living room, cowering and crying if there were any sudden bangs or loud noises. Bridie and her friends never questioned this or spoke to Anna about it; they just knew not to make any loud noises around her dad.

Bridie always knew she could rely on her own father, but was aware that his commitment to God and family wasn't replicated in the homes of some of her friends. Often her schoolfriends had to wait for their dads to roll out of the pub before any wages would be available for food and drink.

In times of poverty there were various dodgy dealings, and for some women that meant prostitution. Although Bridie never knew any sex workers, there were houses in the community that were known to be used for this purpose, and the kids were told to stay away from these places. Bridie was never allowed to play at the home of one schoolfriend, as her mother was rumoured to be a 'working girl'. The neighbours were disgusted to see men traipsing up their closes to this house after the pub had shut. Nevertheless, the darkness of this divided city couldn't eclipse the light and warmth of the McGeown family.

There were other dubious characters who hung around on street corners, namely the men who had made a livelihood during the war by supplying whatever the community needed. There were shops open by this point, but the 'black marketeers' still gathered on street corners in their grey trench coats and caps. These men were able to get hold of pretty much anything people needed at just the right price. They were usually harmless guys who were just looking to make a living, even if their wares often came off the back of a lorry!

A familiar sight across the country at this time was the rag-and-bone man, who would walk around the streets pushing a wheelbarrow and asking for people's unwanted clothing and bric-a-brac. Much to Christine's dismay, four-year-old Joe traded all his best clothes for a balloon one day. She chased the rag-and-bone man down the street until he eventually gave them back, but Joe was deeply upset not to be able to keep his balloon.

Illness often resulted in lengthy spells in hospital or at a sanitorium at this time, and one of Bridie's neighbours, Mr Cowan, spent about eight months in hospital with tuberculosis; a disease that claimed the lives of many. It was a desperate time for his family as he was unable to bring any money in, and there was only so much his wife could do. Once again, the community rallied round so the little family didn't starve.

One woman in the street had terrible bandy legs caused by rickets, a disease that was very common at the time due to poor nutrition and a lack of vitamin D and calcium. Another familiar sight was people with club feet who had to wear platform-soled shoes on one foot and an ordinary shoe on the other, which gave them a permanent limp and left them open to ridicule. Bridie might have suffered this fate had it not been for the careful devotion of her father. The toes on one of her feet were bent right back when she was born, and the foot was very misshapen. The hospital staff told John and Christine to bring her back when she was three and that they would see what they could do, but she would most likely have a club foot and require the special built-up shoes.

John was having none of this, and every night he would come in from work, wash his hands and gently massage Bridie's little foot with his hands and some warm olive oil. He would lovingly manipulate her toes into the correct position, night after night. He did this for the full three years and made her walk up and down the kitchen floor for hours, ensuring that she was putting her foot down flat and that her toes were properly positioned. She would cry about it every night and beg him not to make her do it, but John was determined to give his Bunty the best possible chance of avoiding a club foot.

When she was taken back to the hospital aged three the staff refused to accept it was the same child, as they had never seen such an incredible recovery. While this was wonderful for Bridie, countless other kids without such a devoted father were left disabled for life, perhaps unnecessarily.

Some large families experienced serious overcrowding, and Bridie recalls not being allowed inside one of her friend's houses, always having to wait for her on the doorstep. One time the little girl took Bridie inside while her mother was out, and Bridie immediately noticed there was no bed in the bedroom, which meant they simply put mattresses down on the floor at night as a way of preserving much-needed space during the day. Later on, many people had a versatile cabinet, which hid the bedframe inside and could be tucked away in the daytime. There were homes in which coats were used for duvets, where there were no curtains at the windows and where shoes with no soles were worn, as poverty and unemployment continued to cast a shadow over many communities across the UK.

Like many of the kids in her street, Bridie received free school meals, even during the summer holidays, and she remembers all the children gathering at a local hall to eat their lunch. There was no stigma attached, as everyone in need received them.

Although Bridie's home was harmonious and loving, this wasn't the case for some of her neighbours. Children would called all adults 'aunty' or 'uncle' at this time as a mark of respect. Aunty Jeannie was a very large, rotund woman who lived directly across the street from the McGeowns with her elderly mother. Bridie adored her, but Jeannie wasn't exactly mild-mannered with everyone in the neighbourhood. She certainly didn't see eye to eye with Mrs Malley who lived in the same street.

There were often heated exchanges at the local bookies, and men would come rolling out onto the street together, prompting cries of "Fight, fight!" to echo around the closes and causing a stampede to the windows and close stairwells. One particular Friday night the cry went up and Bridie raced to the window to see which of the men were scrapping, only to find that it was Aunty Jeannie and Mrs Malley rolling about in the street, pulling each other's hair and scratching one another's faces. Aunty Jeannie was calling Mrs Malley very unpleasant names as they tore lumps out of each other. Bridie found this hysterical, especially hearing her call Mrs Malley fat, as it took about four children to get their arms all the way around Aunty Jeannie for a hug! Eventually, some of the men separated the two women, much to Jeannie's disgust.

Transport links at this time were limited. Like the rest of Glasgow, the Gorbals had a tram system that took people where they needed to go when feet or bikes couldn't, only they didn't run at night. Bridie suffered from frequent abscesses in her ears as a child, and one cold, snowy December she woke up in the middle of the night screaming in agony. There was no alternative for John and Christine other than to get her to the nearest hospital, Glasgow Victoria Infirmary. Despite the dark and cold, Christine put Bridie on her back and carried her all three miles to the hospital. Her mother was so comforting and reassuring as she walked through the snow, determined to get her daughter the treatment she needed.

The hospital staff treated the abscess and gave Bridie some pain relief. Then Christine had to turn around and walk the three miles home, protecting her precious daughter all the while. As a treat for being so brave, Bridie was taken to the huge John Lewis department store in the centre of Glasgow the following day, where she was allowed to meet Father Christmas. She had her picture taken on Santa's knee with a balaclava covering the big cotton wool pad on her ear!

The Gorbals of Glasgow may have had its gangsters and troublemakers, its poverty and ill health, but that was never how Bridie saw the world. She thoroughly enjoyed her childhood, and what might now be considered hardship was simply life back then. Stabbings, knife fights, racketeering, organised crime and the like may have been happening in the next street, but all Bridie knew was that the honest, hard-working, kindhearted folks in her world were protecting her from it all. She may not have grown up in a bubble of privilege, but she was raised in a community of family members, friends, 'aunties' and 'uncles' who made sure her childhood remained safe, whatever the external dangers might have been. And for anyone who tried to cause harm there was an army of rolling-pin-wielding mothers ready to strike!

CHAPTER 3:
Celtic Connections

Some of the happiest days of Bridie's childhood were spent in Northern Ireland. Summers were spent at her Aunt Madeleine and Uncle John's place in Portadown, County Armagh, where John and Christine originally hailed from. Bridie has fond memories of the long, sunny days and sticky nights, trying to sleep and stop giggling. It felt more like a homecoming than a holiday. The children were free to run around the countryside and had a couple of new playmates in the shape of their cousins, Roisin and Eugene.

The excitement the children felt was echoed by their parents, who still felt a strong sense of belonging to the land they had emigrated from but never really left. John and Christine seemed so relaxed and carefree in Ireland, and the family enjoyed picnics and trips to the local shops with the many relatives who came to visit.

It was during one of those long, hot summers that ten-year-old Bridie met a certain Michael "Mick" McGoldrick. She wasn't particularly impressed by him back then, but that was to change in later life! Mick's mother had died when he was just eight. His father had moved away with the three eldest children, Anna, Jim and Helena, while the youngest, Tony, was taken to live with his father's cousin and Mick was sent to live at his Aunt Lizzy and Uncle Mick's. Although they made sure he was washed, dressed and fed, it was a loveless environment for Mick to grow up in, and his aunt was often harsh and unreasonable. There was never any spare cash or treats, and Mick grew up isolated from the love and laughter he might have expected as a child with four siblings. Years later he discovered his father had sent him money every month, but he never received a penny of it.

Bridie was at her aunt and uncle's house when Mick appeared on another hazy summer's day. She was in her early teens by this time and had just been given some money because she had found a ring and returned it to her aunt, which meant she had half a crown burning a hole in her pocket. Mick asked her to go to the pictures with him, and they watched The African Queen with Humphrey Bogart and Katharine Hepburn. He asked her years later what would have happened if he had put his arm around her, as he had been desperate to do, and she told him sweetly she would have broken it had he dared. The sentiment may have changed years later, but that candidness never left her!

Whether she was on holiday in Northern Ireland or back home in Glasgow, family always came first and the siblings remained the best of friends. Margaret and Bridie had their own friends and sometimes fought like cat and dog, but they were always close. The boys were also tight; constantly looking out for each other but always up to something. They all had plenty of freedom providing they had done their chores and abided by the family rules. Adventure and experience were encouraged, but their ever-watchful father made sure they toed the line.

Glasgow is home to a vibrant, colourful mix of artists and con artists; a place where brutality and compassion, love and sorrow live side by side. Bridie's personality reflects this diversity. One minute she is the strong, inspiring woman who has conquered suffering with love, the next she is fragile and vulnerable; a woman whose life tapestry displays the woven threads of sorrow and loss. Quiet time has always been important to Bridie. This sociable, engaging woman benefits from a battery recharge and a time of contemplation She can be the life and soul of the party when folks are around, but she truly values her time alone, which she spends talking with God and lingering over memories of those who have gone before her, of whom there have been many.

Bridie would read aloud to her siblings and make up stories to amuse and enthral them, usually in the bedroom she shared with Margaret around a flickering fire. She loved making up adventure stories with each of her siblings in a starring role. They would be pirates, soldiers, princesses, teachers, magicians and many other fantastically imagined heroes, but there was always a happy ending… and they were always home in time for tea!

Although the family wasn't particularly musical, Joe had a talent for playing instruments while the rest sang along. He was also a good impressionist, and the children would beg him to do hilarious impressions of their mum when she wasn't around. Bridie also has a gift for mimicking people and a nifty line in accents, but her main talent was keeping the brood locked in expectant silence as she brought her imaginary characters to life. One of her primary school teachers ignited this love for engaging everyone in the room with words and for taking them on a journey using her vivid imagination. If her life hadn't followed the path it did, those who know her could easily have imagined the talented Bridie on the stage.

Although she took her Catholic teaching seriously – striving to be good, honest and kind – Bridie found herself repeatedly lying to save face as a girl. Her father was nineteen years older than her mother, and the other kids noticed this. On the rare occasions he came to collect her from school or attend an event she pretended he was her grandpa. Although she wasn't ashamed of her beloved father, Bridie didn't want to stick out or be different. That universal need to be as accepted by her peers was as powerful a force in the fifties as it is today.

It's difficult now to imagine Bridie as anything other than confident, such is the strength of her character and appetite for effecting change, yet she has struggled with self-esteem issues over the years. Children are often the cruellest comrades, so even though she hated lying she wasn't prepared to suffer endless teasing for the sake of the truth.

Bridie also harboured deep concerns for her parents, constantly fearing they were about to die. She hated it when they weren't all together at night. One time the chapel boiler broke and the furnace went out. John was the caretaker, so at 10pm he disappeared off into the cold and dark to make sure it was back on for the priests in the morning. Bridie couldn't sleep until he got home because her fertile imagination had gone into overdrive.

Unfortunately, real life was worse than her imagination at times. On one occasion John was jumped on his way back from the chapel and brutally beaten. His attackers ripped his ear off, then stole his money and the chapel keys. John was rushed to hospital and his ear was sewn back on, but it was awful for the family as they waited at home for news of their beloved father. John's most pressing concern was the keys, and he waited up all night so he could be at the priests' door first thing in the morning to apologise. He felt responsible and even offered to take the price of the new keys out of his wages; an offer the priests refused.

The horror of that attack might have had a greater impact had John not demonstrated the fortitude of an ox. The men of Glasgow were considered fortunate to have any form of employment at this time, and the onus was on them to keep their jobs at all costs. John's exemplary work ethic and serving attitude is reflected in Bridie, who often pushes herself to the limit to complete a task.

At the age of eleven Bridie contracted pleurisy and was off school for a full year. Rather than missing out on any education, her bedroom doubled up as a classroom, with both parents proving to be willing teachers. The young student avidly read her books and completed the work that was sent home from school. She also benefited from the vast personal knowledge of her loving tutors, who patiently explained how things worked and shared experiences from their own lives. Whether it was English, arithmetic, geography, history or science, Bridie was keen to learn, and her little mind was like a sponge that soaked up everything she was taught or read. The other kids also took part, and despite her pain and frailty Bridie enjoyed her small, familiar school. There was a great deal of laughter as a bossy Margaret became headmistress to her bedridden sibling!

The time was clearly well spent, as Bridie sat her end-of-year exam on her first day back and passed with flying colours. Her teachers must have felt slightly perturbed at the result, given that she had received none of their input during that time. It helped that she was highly intelligent with a keen interest in history and current affairs. She still has an opinion on everything that makes the news today and an insatiable thirst for knowledge.

School continued to be of great interest to Bridie. She spent her days in the classroom soaking up as much information as she could and thriving on the strict routines and harsh conditions, with freezing classrooms in the winter and sweltering heat in the summer. She loved having the freedom to meet up with her friends and to play games with skipping ropes and balls. She was an above-average student and took her work seriously, handing in her homework on time and respecting all her teachers… even the less engaging ones.

As she grew older, she loved to learn about other countries and different people groups, especially as travelling to far-flung places seemed an impossible dream at that time. She loved discussing what she had learned in English and History with her parents, who encouraged all their children to try their best, even if they didn't like the subject. And so her teenage years continued: doing well at school, enjoying her home life, and most of all loving those long, lively holidays in Northern Ireland.

CHAPTER 4:
If The Shoe Fits

Bridie's schooldays were drawing to a close, and at this time girls were not encouraged to pursue a career. Instead, they were directed into housekeeping and cooking while the boys learned a trade. Given the chance, Bridie would have loved to be an interior designer, and judging by her beautifully co-ordinated home she would almost certainly have excelled at it, but sadly that wasn't an option.

Having left school one Friday afternoon, fifteen-year-old Bridie began her retail career at Carr's shoe shop on the Saturday morning, which happened to be just around the corner from home. Having barely slept the night before, she entered the shop with a racing pulse and a stomach full of butterflies. Bridie needn't have worried, however, as once inside she instantly felt at ease and ready to embrace this new chapter of her life. She wore a huge green overall that trailed around her ankles, beneath which was her black school skirt and a crisp white blouse. The new look made her feel very grown up, and she loved the leathery smell of the shop.

The boss was a formidable woman called Miss McGeehan, whose strict and efficient manner terrified young Bridie. As a new starter she wasn't initially allowed to sell the shoes; she was merely tasked with keeping the place tidy and running to fetch anything Miss McGeehan required from the stockroom. Bridie rose to every challenge she was given and was a great asset to the shop. She quickly offered to help with the bookkeeping, and within weeks was doing the books all by herself. She often stayed behind after hours to help make sure the accounts were ready to send to head office. Miss McGeehan appreciated the help, and Bridie not only enjoyed but was adept at it, which was fortunate seeing as it turned out to be a skill she would rely on later in life.

Not everybody was happy with the extra responsibility Bridie had been given, however. Aged just seventeen, she was about to be handed the keys to run the shop while Miss McGeehan went on holiday one particular night. Suddenly, the door was chapped, and in came Bridie's father. He glanced at Miss McGeehan, then turned to Bridie and told her to get her coat, making it abundantly clear that the working day was over. Bridie immediately obeyed and left the shop, and Miss McGeehan never let her stay so late again. After this incident, a love for employees' rights was birthed within Bridie.

Bridie received the princely sum of two pounds and two shillings as her wages. She gave it all to her mother as soon as she received it each week but always got the two shillings back for herself. This practice of handing over her wages to her mother continued each week until she left home several years later.

Eventually, she was allowed to sell the shoes and Bridie took to it like the proverbial duck to water, watching her mentor closely and carrying out her duties meticulously. Always keen to learn a new skill and perform it well, Bridie put all she had observed leading up to that moment to good use and made sure she was particularly adept at not only selling but also upselling.

It wasn't long before Bridie learned that her boss had a far softer side. If customers didn't have enough cash they could pay with a Caledonian, Bristol or Provident cheque, commonly known as a 'Caley', 'Bristol' or 'Provy'. These were a forerunner of payday loans, as people would take out an agreement with the provider and then pay the sum back at a high rate of interest. If a family Miss McGeehan knew and trusted needed shoes but payday wasn't for a few days she would let them have the shoes anyway, trusting they would come in on the Friday to settle up. Bridie loved this about her manager, and, after spending a fair amount of time in the shop herself, she learned who could be trusted and who couldn't. Although they were no soft touches, both women were full of compassion and kindness, which was greatly appreciated in the Gorbals community.

Bridie's desire to help those in need was evident even during this early stage of her life, but there was one occasion when she didn't rely on her softer side. A middle-aged family man had called in three times to collect a pair of shoes for his daughter, which were being repaired. The shoes had been sent to head office in Edinburgh, so there had been a delay. When Miss McGeehan told him they still weren't back, he lunged forward and grabbed her.

Quick as a flash, Bridie jumped over the counter and onto the man's back, pummelling him with her fists and screaming at him to leave Miss McGeehan alone. The man's wife just stood there, looking absolutely gobsmacked, and the husband got quite the fright as well. He stopped in his tracks and said, "Lassie, I'm so sorry. Please don't be afraid. My wee girl has no more shoes to wear, and I got desperate. I'm so sorry." Bridie was shaking so much afterwards that Miss McGeehan sent for her mother, and the young shop assistant was taken home for the afternoon. Many years on, no one messes with her!

It wasn't all hardship at the shop, and Bridie enjoyed having first pick of the goods and the generous staff discount. You can almost smell the leather and whitening as Bridie shares her memories of a bygone era when fashion was reserved for the young adults while the children had to wear whatever they were told.

Working in a busy shop meant Bridie was able to stay up to date with the latest trends, and she loved being able to choose her own accessories. Although the times may have been tough and money restricted, style was not! After the lace-up sandshoe fashion came the slip-on. Every teenage girl wanted slip-ons, and those who had a pair considered themselves very classy. Bridie also loved the smart crepe soles the Teddy Boys wore, and as the soles lasted ages most mothers were happy for their sons to wear them. It also made the boys look taller, which boosted their popularity. Cuban-heeled boots came next, then Cuban-heeled shoes, and Bridie was in her element fitting and selling the latest, if not always greatest, footwear to her local community.

There was one strange yet familiar sight on window ledges across Glasgow every Saturday night, and it wasn't plant pots but plimsolls! The shoe shops sold white ones for girls and black for the boys. On Saturdays they were duly cleaned and the girls' were whitened, and then they would all be left out to dry on the sills for chapel the next morning.

Footwear, and indeed fashion in general, was bold and daring at this time. Next came winkle-pickers for the men, which were especially popular among those who belonged to gangs as well as those leading the dancing at weekend socials during the heady days of rock-and-roll and big-band music. Next for women came a shoe that has been loved and hated in equal measure over the years: the stiletto! Any girl who had heels and a miniskirt was the height of fashion at this time. Bags were also used as fashion statements, and baskets were all the rage. Bridie loved the pretty straw baskets Carr's sold, and owned several of them herself.

One shoe brand that was particularly popular among the working-class men of the day was TUF. The shoes came with a twelve-month guarantee that shopkeepers had to honour. Some crafty families would share one pair between two people. If one worked a day shift and the other a night shift, the shoes would be passed back and forth. Everybody had them – bus drivers, posties, shipyard workers, the lot – and they all made sure they got their new pair if they didn't last the full year!

When Bridie was thirteen or fourteen her brothers were still wearing short trousers. They all had hobnail boots, which Bridie would beg to borrow as they were brilliant for sliding down the street in. She was a wonderful mix of sophisticated young woman and daredevil tomboy.

The McGeown presence at Carr's soon doubled with the arrival of Margaret two years after Bridie had joined the ranks. By this point Bridie was flying in her job, sometimes serving around twelve customers at a time. She loved seeing satisfied people leave the shop but also tried to ensure that each sale benefited her. She made 6p commission for selling Utility shoes, so those were the ones she pushed the hardest. She often managed to sell a pair of red or blue Utility shoes to someone who had come in asking for black patent school shoes!

Bridie occasionally felt she had to resort to a certain amount of trickery, as folks would often ask her to fix their shoes, complaining they were too tight. The staff kept a broom out the back that they nicknamed Iain. Whenever anyone came in with shoes that pinched Bridie or one of the others would explain that there was a guy called Iain who fixed things out the back. Then they would go through, stand around for five minutes doing nothing, shout "Thank you!" to Iain the shoe-fixer, then go back to the customer and say they had been stretched and should now be fine. Off the customer went believing the shoes had been fixed!

More often than not, however, Bridie would go the extra mile as many of her customers were in dire straits and she knew they sometimes had no money to put shoes on their kids' feet. One day a big giant of a man came in with a cheque the shop shouldn't have taken, but Bridie could see he was desperate. There were tears in his eyes as he explained his little girl had no shoes to wear and he wasn't leaving until he had a pair. He said he would do odd jobs – anything that might be needed – just to make sure his daughter had something to wear. Bridie didn't care about protocol; she simply took the cheque and gave him the shoes he needed. It impacted her deeply to see the man's poverty and loss of pride, and she never forgot the encounter. She felt a great sympathy for this father who had been so humbled by lack through no fault of his own.

Unfortunately, Margaret didn't share Bridie's dedication or the pride she took in her work; in fact, she spent more time avoiding work than actually doing it. Thinking up ways to ensure that her sister earned her wages, Bridie asked Margaret to go the bank one morning, thinking the extra responsibility would encourage her sister to be more industrious. The plan backfired, because although the bank was only two streets away Margaret managed to disappear until closing time! The pair had great fun in the shop together, however, and once again Bridie provided a rich source of entertainment on quiet afternoons. She would do impressions and make up stories about customers and reps, sending Margaret into fits of giggles. The pair often had to hide out the back until they had calmed down.

Their elder brother John had qualified as a butcher and worked just across the road, so the three of them often walked home together. They all finished at 1pm on Tuesday afternoons, so they would head back early and keep themselves busy at home. A few disapproving folks aside, there was a strong sense of togetherness and unity in the Gorbals, and community spirit was unwavering. The McGeowns may not have been exposed to the harshest brutalities in the area, but they very much felt as though everyone was in it together and had each other's backs.

CHAPTER 5:
Two Become One ...
Two ... Three

The McGeowns' summers continued to be spent in Ireland. Bridie loved staying at her Aunt Madeleine and Uncle John's place in Portadown, especially as the handsome young Mick McGoldrick was firmly on the scene by the time Bridie was seventeen. Mick was eighteen by this point and young love was in the air.

She had just arrived one Sunday when, together with her cousins, she bumped into Mick and his friend at the local park. Bridie pretended she didn't know how to load the film in her camera so she had an excuse to talk to him. Mick had no idea how to load it but ran off to see someone and get it done, insisting she take a picture of him when he returned with it. She was more than happy to comply!

But Mick couldn't rely solely on his charm and chivalry. Given that she was known as the city girl from Scotland, Bridie was a source of great interest and all the local boys were buzzing around her like flies, much to Master McGoldrick's disgust. Mick already had a date for the dance that night, but he decided to go alone instead. He glared at every lad who asked Bridie to dance until he eventually plucked up the courage to ask himself. Staring into his bright blue eyes for the first time sent shivers down Bridie's spine. She knew then that this young man was going to be very special to her.

At the end of the night he asked to walk her home, and she agreed. However, Mick was a little too countrified for Bridie, making her wait outside the venue while he ran to get his bike so he could cycle home after escorting her back to her uncle's house. Pushing it along beside him as they talked, Bridie felt embarrassed at first because no city boy back home would have been seen dead doing such a thing, but she quickly got over it as she started to enjoy his company. The night ended even more embarrassingly when, after spending a long time chatting about anything and everything outside the house, the night came to an abrupt end when Uncle John shouted out the window that it was time for her to come in!

Bridie's cousin Roisin made her the very first standout petticoat she had ever owned; a lovely undergarment with several layers of material that filled out her dress and made it swing beautifully from side to side when she moved. Bridie felt extremely grown up wearing it when her beau took her to Warrenpoint for high tea, which he had saved up his full two weeks' wages at Tavanagh Weaving Factory to pay for. Although his home life had been pretty bleak at times, Mick had grown up to be a happy, fun-loving person with a very generous heart.

Bridie spent almost the full two weeks of her holiday in Mick's company, and even back then she knew Mick was the man for her. Having initially fallen in love with his eyes, she soon got to know him as a person. She loved everything about him and hated saying goodbye at the end of each holiday. He came to the train station to see her off at the end of her visit and felt completely broken-hearted as he saw her disappearing off into the distance.

Mick had asked Bridie to write to him, but Bridie was adamant that he should write first. He happily obliged, sending the first letter in June 1960. The couple wrote to each other every single day they were apart, which happened to be a great deal over the next three years. Receiving a handwritten letter was a wonderful way to keep a relationship alive and discover more about one another. This was far more than a summer romance and everyone around them knew it.

Meanwhile, life as Bridie had always known it in Glasgow was about to change forever. Her beloved big brother Joe had decided to join the RAF and Bridie was devastated. Coming from such a close family, and having felt so happy and secure growing up in one another's company, this was hard to take. Bridie was reluctant to enter this new phase of life, and in some ways it felt like a death. The whole family wept buckets as an excited Joe went away for his training, ready to embrace a great adventure.

No sooner had the family begun to adjust to this change when Pat made the decision to travel down to London to take a job as a train driver. He sent money home every week, and Bridie's imagination went into overdrive as she thought about her brother, the young prankster from the Gorbals, driving around the capital city past Marble Arch, Buckingham Palace, Westminster and all the exciting areas she had heard about but only ever dreamed of visiting.

His departure was a further bitter blow, and Bridie couldn't believe another of her fun-loving siblings was moving away. She wanted her brother to be happy, and the bright lights of London seemed enticing, but she couldn't believe he had also left the nest. Pat had always worshipped Christine, and, while she did her best to stay upbeat in front of the children, their mother desperately missed his familiar fun and chatter around the house.

Although these moves were a natural part of family life and the best decisions for both young men, there was a sense that the family was becoming fractured as the children went their separate ways, and Bridie didn't like it at all. The dinner table at the McGeowns' place was suddenly much quieter.

Bridie gradually adjusted to life without her brothers. The daily letters she received from a certain blue-eyed charmer in Northern Ireland and the calls she took on the phone box in the next street helped to ease her pain. The pair were deeply in love and dreamed of spending more time together; so much so that Mick eventually made the massive decision to leave his beloved homeland to be nearer.

With all his worldly belongings in hand, Mick moved to Birmingham. But while Bridie admired the fact he had upped sticks to be close to her, it wasn't really much nearer. He still needed to take several buses and trains to see her, a fact she never tired of teasing him about. Nevertheless, Mick was as sweet and funny as ever, and their calls and letters always contained a great deal of humour.

Like so many young men at this time, Mick decided to enlist in the army shortly after moving to Birmingham. He joined the Royal Engineers and was stationed in Germany. It was quite a challenge for Bridie to know that her boyfriend was abroad, and even worse that he could be called up if there was another war. She tried not to think about that possibility. As far as she was concerned he was just away learning a trade and earning some money. Mick never really thought of the army as a career path, and he didn't want to spend his whole life serving as a soldier, but he wanted to be earning. It was tough not being able to get together whenever they wanted, but the enforced absence made their time together sweeter whenever Mick was on leave.

The love-struck pair continued their correspondence, and Bridie lived for the moment the postman arrived with her precious letter. One morning when Bridie was eighteen a registered letter arrived, carrying more than just the usual chat and sweet nothings. On the outside of the envelope Mick had written: "Let's join the Shamrock and Thistle together and see what happens." On the inside was a beautiful engagement ring: a sapphire stone surrounded by diamonds and set within a gold heart. She absolutely loved it.

Bridie couldn't believe her good fortune, and of course she wrote back to say yes. She refused to put the ring on, however, as she wanted to wait until he was there to pop the question and place the ring on her finger in person. Mick was everything Bridie had ever wanted in a husband, and she started counting down the days until they could make their engagement official.

The next time Mick was home on leave, Bridie became engaged to the man of her dreams at the ripe old age of eighteen. She immediately took to flashing her left hand with its beautiful adornment whenever she could. Life hadn't really changed for the young couple, except that they both wore even bigger lovestruck grins. Bridie had never been more sure of anything. She wanted to marry this man and stay with him for the rest of her life.

Mick came home as often as possible and the pair continued to write daily. Bridie was still working at Carr's, fitting the feet of her local community and helping out at home. These were happy times for the young couple. It was really important to Bridie that her parents and the rest of the gang were happy for them, but she needn't have worried, as Mick was loved by everyone in the family. He was the kind of person nobody ever had a bad word to say about, and even into his sixties his deep, mesmerising blue eyes still shone with love for Bridie.

On 22nd May 1963, two years after their engagement and just two days before Mick's twenty-first birthday, the happy couple were married in Glasgow. It wasn't a straightforward process, however. The pair needed to have several documents signed before they could proceed: a form from Mick's commanding officer, a letter from his father because he was under twenty-one and a letter of freedom signed by every parish Mick had belonged to. The army was slow in getting the forms signed, and the night before the wedding the priest who was marrying the couple still hadn't received them. Everyone breathed a huge sigh of relief when they arrived the morning of the wedding, though the priest commented that as they were such a nice, respectable couple he would have married them anyway.

There was much bustle and excitement in the family home as everyone got ready for the big day, which was to kick off at ten o'clock in Glasgow. There were clothes, shoes and bags galore as the blushing bride prepared to leave her family home as a single woman for the last time. Bridie was so happy and certain, but that didn't stop the excitement reaching fever pitch as the time for the ceremony approached.

Everyone eventually set off for the chapel, leaving Bridie and her dad behind. John wasn't usually an emotional man, but he took his daughter's hands in his, looked into her eyes and asked if she was sure she wanted to go ahead. Bridie assured him she had never been more certain of anything in her life. Mick McGoldrick was the man for her and she wanted nothing more than to be his wife. Her father smiled and simply squeezed his beloved Bunty's hand in response. There was no big, impassioned Hollywood-style speech, but this was all Bridie needed to feel her father's love, protection, honour and joy.

She and Mick exchanged vows at the chapel, then took the forms up to the registry office in Martha Street to make it official. After that they went back to John and Christine's, where family members and friends enjoyed a lovely wedding breakfast in Bridie's beloved family kitchen. After this they were to head down to the docks to board the ship that would take them to their two-week honeymoon destination in Warrenpoint, Northern Ireland.

This wasn't a simple farewell, however, as Christine kept delaying them by making endless cups of tea and trying to keep the newlyweds chatting every time they tried to leave the house. The pair eventually managed to free themselves from the strangely clingy Christine only to discover that she had been buying time so the whole family could get down to the docks to wave them off. Bridie's face still reddens when she thinks back to them being showered in confetti and covered in hugs and lipstick as they made their way to their onboard cabin. They immediately became known to the other passengers as "the wee honeymoon couple". She may not have enjoyed all the attention of the send-off, but Bridie soon found she couldn't live without the attentions of her new husband. Being married to Mick was a dream come true, and the new Mrs McGoldrick was on cloud nine, ready for the many adventures that lay ahead.

Mick and Bridie spent their honeymoon in a wonderful old railway carriage that had been converted into a caravan, and they loved every minute of it. The campsite was quiet in May with very little entertainment, so, ever-resourceful, the couple decided to hitchhike to nearby Rostrevor one evening to watch a film at the local cinema. All went well on the way there, and they enjoyed the movie. However, the return journey wasn't quite so comfortable, as they hitched a ride in an old rickety van with Bridie sitting on Mick's knee and Mick holding the door shut as the handle was broken. Although they appreciated the kindness of the man who had stopped for them, they couldn't wait to get out!

Nevertheless, the pair had a great laugh throughout their stay. The people in Warrenpoint were so kind and considerate, and everyone seemed happy to help the newlyweds. They certainly made the most of those first two weeks together after the long absences they had endured as an unmarried couple. The joy of their marital union was even sweeter following their chaste and traditional courtship. She just knew that everything would be fine so long as she was with her Mick. Bridie loved the wonderful way he had of seeing the good in everything and believing the best in others. He was also great fun to be around, and the pair laughed constantly, always happy to be in each other's company. She knew she had married well and delighted in telling everyone she met all about it.

Sadly, the honeymoon couldn't last forever. The pair returned to Bridie's family home in Glasgow before Mick headed down to Ripon, where he was stationed at the time. Bridie was still living in her family home and working with Margaret at the shoe shop. She was very content with her life, though sad that she had to be separated from her husband again. The familiar communication pattern emerged once more, with Bridie receiving a letter from her beloved every morning and writing her response every night.

Mick was able to travel back to Glasgow every weekend at first, but after six months he was posted to Aden in Egypt (now part of Yemen). The separation was hard on both of them, and Bridie was heartbroken as she wasn't even able to hear his voice while he was there. Mick hated being apart from his young bride just as much as she did.

After six months he was given leave and the pair were absolutely ecstatic to see each other again. Bridie was determined to look her best, booking a hairdresser's appointment for the afternoon and seeking out her best clothes. Nothing was too much trouble as she planned how the day would go. She desperately wanted to wow him when he saw her. True to form, however, Mick surprised her by arriving home on the Sunday morning to find his bride in her nightgown with no make-up or fancy hairdo. She squealed with delight and embarrassment as she ran into the arms of her husband!

It wasn't quite the romantic reunion she had dreamed of, as her parents, John, Frank and Margaret were all home that morning. Mick was absolutely freezing, having travelled up alone on the overnight carriage with no heating to get there as quickly as possible, so a great fuss was made of him. The fire was lit, warm food was placed on the table for him and the whole house rang with laughter as Bridie's soldier husband held her snugly in his arms.

On one occasion Mick travelled up after a twenty-four-hour shift, looking for a bit of intimacy with his wife. He arrived at 1.30pm on a Tuesday afternoon to surprise her, thinking it would be good to catch her alone, only to discover that the whole family was there once again. After a nice hot meal and a good chat he turned around and hitchhiked back to base. Instead of an amorous tryst with his sweetheart, Mick ended up with a full stomach and a chat with the in-laws! They laughed about this for years afterwards.

John loved Mick but tore strips off his son-in-law when they came back from an evening with friends after 11pm one time. In those times, women weren't often out and about that late and it could harm her reputation if she was. John strongly objected to Mick keeping his daughter out until such an hour. Mick protested that they had only been a few doors along having a perfectly innocent time, and even reminded John that he was Bridie's husband. This didn't go down well, however. John made it clear that while she might be Mick's wife Bridie would always be his daughter, and Mick was never to disrespect her like that again. As ever, Bridie saw the funny side of it and stayed up in the bedroom shaking with uncontrollable laughter while Mick got his ticking off!

Another time, Bridie's ever-protective father offered her some unsolicited fashion advice. She was heading to the cinema wearing a tight-fitting button-up skirt, which was very much the fashion. John asked where she thought she was going dressed like that and told her there was no way she would be sitting in the cinema in that outfit. A bemused Mick could barely believe his eyes when Bridie dutifully went upstairs to change. She never had any sense that her father was being overbearing or interfering. Bridie was always grateful that she had been brought up by a wonderful man who had high standards and expected his children to be respected and honoured, especially by their spouses.

Mick soon returned to Ripon from Aden and travelled back to Glasgow every second weekend. Shortly after this, Bridie's emotions went into overdrive but she couldn't work out why. She was heading to Felixstowe with Margaret one day to see Joe and his wife and their wee boy, but as she said goodbye to Mick just beforehand her tears were uncontrollable. He was stationed in Cyprus at this point, so he was going to be away for six weeks, and Bridie was so distraught she couldn't stop crying. Christine was concerned about her daughter, but Bridie insisted she was fine. She just hated the idea of going back to letter-writing once more.

Bridie was aware that something felt different, but she wasn't sure what. Soon after this she realised she had missed a period and went to the doctor. It turned out she was pregnant, and Bridie was delighted. She immediately sent Mick a letter before telling her ecstatic parents. There were more tears as Bridie would rather have told her husband the news face to face, but this wasn't enough to spoil her happiness. It was a dream come true, and she felt such joy as she considered what the future would hold for them and their child.

Chapter 6:
Pitter Patter

Bridie was rather surprised when Mick didn't reply to her letter or mention the pregnancy in subsequent communications. The next time he came home she asked why he hadn't responded to the big news. He asked what the news was, as her letter had never arrived, so she was able to tell him he was going to be a daddy face to face after all. Bridie was delighted and made a big deal of imparting the wonderful news. Mick, however, was suspended in disbelief, repeatedly asking if she was sure and looking quizzically at her flat stomach. He eventually admitted that he thought pregnant women became huge immediately, which amused Bridie no end. After a bit of explanation and reassurance, Mick accepted the truth that they were going to be parents. The pair looked like a couple of Cheshire cats as they imagined the joy that was to come. Bridie instinctively knew Mick would make a wonderful dad, as he was always so loving and caring.

Nevertheless, the young soldier had to return to normal army life and the letter-writing resumed once again. The couple continued to express their undying love for one another and Bridie assured Mick that she and their unborn baby were doing well. At this point Bridie and Mick were given their own council house to rent, which just happened to be across the road from her parents' place. As Mick was away, Bridie had to view the house and accept it on her own, but she knew her husband would approve.

Mick always gave generously to folks in need, and Bridie quickly learned never to question the logic behind it. They were out walking one evening shortly after she had fallen pregnant when they saw a really shabby-looking guy begging. Mick put some money in the man's hat, but Bridie could see that he intended to buy alcohol with it. When she mentioned this to Mick and questioned why he would give the money regardless, Mick said it wasn't up to them to tell someone what to buy with their gifts. He reminded her that God gives the gift of his love and his Son to all unconditionally. Bridie was really struck by this and always respected his financial decisions from this point on.

Despite all her strength and determination, Bridie had one area of weakness. She was terrified of hospitals, so she elected for a home birth. The midwife and doctor were all on board for when the baby was due, and much to her delight Mick made it home in time. However, this soldier who had gallantly served his country with bravery and distinction proved to be a little less heroic during the birth of his first child. Normally laidback, he was as nervous as a kitten and extremely anxious; so much so that the doctor had to give him a sedative, much to Bridie's amusement.

Fathers weren't made welcome during the delivery in those days, so Mick stayed outside the room with Bridie's equally fractious father. Her labour began on the Tuesday morning, and after taking the sedative Mick calmed down and went off to clean the gas cooker for something to do. The labour lasted three full days, by which time Mick had the entire house sparkling. Meanwhile, John was pacing up and down the street, telling everyone he met that his daughter was in labour. It became quite the community affair, with everyone feeling great concern for Bridie.

Mick stopped his cleaning on the Friday to meet their beautiful son, Michael John McGoldrick, who had been born at 11.43am weighing 8lbs. It had been an exceedingly difficult birth, but holding him in their arms, safe and sound, was the best feeling the pair had ever experienced.

Michael was a handsome, healthy child, and it was such a wonderful time for the family. They were both ecstatic, but Bridie was exhausted after a wearying and worrying three-day labour. She was sore from head to toe and desperately needed sleep. The whole family was over the moon with Michael, and there was a steady stream of visitors, day and night. The nurse soon put her foot down and insisted there were to be no visitors for forty-eight hours or Bridie never would have had any rest.

Baby Michael had everybody wrapped around his little finger right from the outset, and even as a baby he was very sociable. He loved being held and chatted to, and was all smiles, rather like his doting parents. Meanwhile, Mick took to fatherhood like a duck to water. Bridie walked into the living room one afternoon during the first week and smiled with joy at her husband, who was showing her brother John how to hold the baby and where to place his hands, like an old pro. Mick was so proud of his son and Michael was loving it, as was Bridie as she watched her husband showing off his new parenting skills.

The couple quickly settled into their new life in their new home with their new baby. Although Bridie's family lived just across the road it was good to be able to close the door and have their own space. Mick so enjoyed being a dad and even loved pacing the floor to get Michael to sleep. It didn't help that the baby was so adorable and would snuggle into his daddy's neck while looking up at him with his huge, innocent eyes. Mick and Bridie were completely smitten, and they made the most of every single moment. They enjoyed each little touch, even the dirty nappies and night feeds, but most of all that wonderful baby smell as they cuddled him. Those were precious moments for Bridie, especially as Mick had to return to the army when Michael was just ten days old. He was devastated at having to leave his young family, and Bridie was upset that he was going, but it was the way things were for all young couples in the services.

The night came when Mick had to catch his train down south, and it happened to be the evening of Michael's christening. Bridie was inconsolable. She tried really hard to be strong, but the tears just came flowing down, particularly when she was forced to watch Mick kiss his darling boy goodbye and hand him back to her. It was only temporary, and Mick would be back soon enough, but it seemed like the end of the world at that moment.

Difficult as it was to wave Mick goodbye, Bridie knew she had the loving support of her family on her doorstep, which was more than many other young army wives had. She headed over there straightaway to be comforted. As it turned out, it wasn't only Bridie and little Michael who would be in need of cuddles, as it wasn't long before there were nappies on the washing line at her parents' house once again.

CHAPTER 7:
Baby Talk

The McGeown household expanded further with the birth of Margaret's daughter Christina. Baby Christina was born just four months after Michael, but in vastly different circumstances. Margaret wasn't married to her daughter's father and they didn't stay together. This simply wasn't the done thing during the sixties, so it raised a few eyebrows and fuelled plenty of gossip.

For such a God-fearing family, brought up to follow the rules and rituals of Catholicism, John and Christine might have found it too much to take, but the whole family supported Margaret. There was no shouting, judgement or reproach, nor any question of excluding her; they simply loved her and were as excited and helpful with Margaret as they had been with Bridie. They were there for her throughout the pregnancy and became her support network afterwards.

Margaret felt too ashamed to go out at first, as she knew everyone would be talking about her. But Bridie, fiercely loyal and protective as ever, gave her sister some wise advice and assured her that anyone who had anything to say about her bringing a child into this world to love should come and see her feisty big sister. Anyone who even considered mocking Margaret would have been forced to reconsider at the prospect of facing Bridie's wrath!

Not only had the sisters enjoyed a close childhood, but they had shared the ups and downs of pregnancy as well. Remarkably, they also shared the same aversion to hospitals, so Margaret also had a home birth. Margaret's pain was so bad in the throes of labour that she thought she was dying, but Bridie, her closest ally, friend and sister, remained by her side throughout. The pain increased and Margaret writhed in agony, begging Bridie to bring her orphaned baby up as her own. She was suffering to such an extent that Bridie also became traumatised, so when the healthy baby was eventually born the nurse handed her to Bridie to calm her down.

Margaret had an allergic reaction to penicillin after the birth and became seriously ill, and once again Bridie thought they were going to lose her. She was determined to bring Margaret's baby up as her own and love both children unconditionally. Thankfully, Margaret survived the traumatic labour and allergic reaction, and Bridie still feels an unbreakable bond with Christina. Although ill winds and circumstances have tried to separate them over the years, the two remain as close as ever, and Christina still calls Bridie 'Aunty Bunty' and 'Nana Bo'. Bridie was delighted that she and her sister were to share their happiest moments of early motherhood after all.

Bridie was closest to Margaret and John, who still worked across the road from his sisters in the butcher's, so she asked them to be Michael's godparents. Bridie's ever-caring father asked Bridie if she wanted to stay with them as she was on her own so much, but Bridie said she was fine, knowing they were all just across the street if she needed them. Michael was such an adorable baby she just loved being in her own home with him.

Mick was away for ten weeks on that occasion, and he couldn't wait to get home to see them. Bridie was so excited she ran up the street to meet him. He was more than surprised by how his little boy looked, as he had imagined Michael would be about the same size as when he left. He couldn't believe this growing baby was his son. Once he got over the shock it was like Bridie didn't exist as the excited father threw himself into the role. He did everything he could think of for Michael and spent hours just watching him, even while he was sleeping.

Mick would often say, "Did you see that? He smiled at me" or "Did you see that? He recognised me" or "Did you see that? He likes that". Even after the hundredth time Bridie just had to keep nodding and agreeing. She didn't mind for one minute that her husband was doing everything for Michael; she simply enjoyed spending this precious, fun time with her two boys.

The trio spent time alone as a family and also with Bridie's folks. Mick was loved by everyone and fitted in easily, which was just as well. Like every young couple with a baby they delighted in the simplest things during those early weeks and months, and both enjoyed taking Michael to the park or going out for walks together. Mick was delighted to be at home with his family.

Despite Glasgow's rough reputation back then, Bridie never felt scared or worried for her family. It was her home city and all she had ever known, and to Bridie it was a loving, caring community. She didn't look around at the streets and sprawling tenements and see trouble; she saw neighbours and friends, characters and customers. Like all young mums of the day, Bridie could hardly pass anyone on the street without being given a penny or a sweetie for the 'wean'. It was a happy place to bring up children and she wanted Michael to enjoy the happy, carefree childhood she had experienced.

Mick's leave was always over far too quickly, and he was soon heading southbound on the train again, having waved his little family off at the station. There was one slight problem for the family, in that the baby didn't like seeing his dad in uniform and he let it be known, loudly. Bridie figured it was because Michael was so used to being shown the photo of his dad in uniform that he was confused by the real-life version!

Each time he left, Bridie would watch the train disappear off into the horizon, then push the pram back to her parents' house, where the kettle was always on. Tea and laughter always helped, and the moments she shared around the kitchen table with Margaret and her mum were truly happy ones. The two sisters would go shopping, take the babies to the park and travel into town together, always having fun. Bridie never thought twice about the fact that Margaret was unmarried. They were simply best friends and sisters enjoying their beautiful babies together.

Life as a single mother was tough financially, and before Christina was two months old Margaret had to go back to work, so her mother agreed to watch the baby. Bridie also helped out and happily looked after little Christina, and both babies enjoyed the best attentions of their close-knit community. All the neighbours who had taken an interest in Bridie and Margaret growing up were just as delighted to see them become mothers to their own kids, and there were always plenty of visitors popping in to see the weans.

Bridie loved taking Michael outside and letting him play beside Christina on a rug on a warm day, and she enjoyed seeing her mother caring for babies again. Bridie was as close as ever to Christine and loved this new phase of life in which she could ask her mother endless questions about bringing up her baby, especially seeing as Christine had done such a good job with her own children. Bridie's admiration for her mother went through the roof at this time, as she considered all that she and John had done for them growing up.

Bridie missed her sister while she was at work but was determined to cherish every day with a fast-growing Michael, as she would have to return to work herself when he turned one. Again, it was Christine who stepped up to watch him when the time came, which meant the cousins were still together much of the time. It wasn't just Michael who cried like a baby that first morning, however. Bridie really didn't want to leave him, but she and Mick needed the money. The young mother reluctantly returned to Carr's and working life, even though she spent most of the day sobbing over the shoes.

By the time Michael was eighteen months old, Mick decided he'd had enough of all the comings and goings. Unwilling to miss out on any more of his toddling son's life, the Irishman was determined to be there permanently, so he left the army for the last time. He had many friends, some of whom he had served with for years, but in his heart he had never really wanted to be a soldier anyway. Although he would miss the camaraderie and laughs, Mick McGoldrick left with a spring in his step, racing towards civvy street with a grateful heart.

Bridie was over the moon that their days of separation were over and was so glad to have him home. Mick was also excited to be able to live with them full time and to share Michael's everyday life with her. Once again, Bridie was able to stare into those beautiful blue eyes in person rather than just gazing at photographs. Having a baby had done nothing to dampen the passion and desire she felt for her favourite Irishman.

CHAPTER 8:
Boys To Men

The happy trio soon readjusted to life together. Mick started working as a postman, which Bridie joked was because he missed wearing his army uniform. They were a typical working-class family, with no bath in the house to get rid of all the mud their growing toddler acquired during his daily adventures, but enjoying plenty of love and laughs with the occasional luxury thrown in. Michael thrived with both parents at home, and they all settled into civvy life well.

Michael would plead for his life when it was time for his sink bath each night, or at least for another ten minutes outside. Bridie wished she had said no to extra play time one night, but her little boy was all charm and she agreed to let him have another ten minutes. She used the time to wash her hair, sticking a towel on her head while she waited for him to reappear.

Minutes later, Michael rushed in with his leg burst open and blood dripping everywhere. Bridie and Mick borrowed a pushchair from a neighbour and ran him up to the nearest hospital. They were terrified, but young Michael loved all the attention and played up being severely injured. It wasn't until the couple had given the receptionist his name and address and taken a seat in the waiting room that Bridie realised she still had the wet towel bundled around her wet hair!

Michael had to have his leg stitched up as it was split right down the middle. Bridie was so glad Mick was able to be there with them, even if he wasn't the best at dealing with the situation and eventually gave in to panic and horror. Despite realising it was part and parcel of being a small child, Mick was really angry it had happened. He turned to Bridie when they got home, his face still white with shock, and said, "I never, ever want to hold my child while he's getting stitches again."

Ten days later they went to the doctor's surgery, where a nurse proceeded to take the stitches out. Michael began to scream as his leg opened up. Bridie was insistent that the wound needed longer to heal, but the nurse sent her out of the room, suggesting she was upsetting Michael. Bridie was furious, particularly when her son was still in agony the next day and they had to go back to get the leg drained and the wound restitched.

An irate Bridie complained to the nurse, who happened to be attending to her son again, but she became even angrier when the nurse looked directly at her and told a barefaced lie, denying she had ever taken his stitches out. Nobody believed Bridie, which enraged her as she saw the mess Michael's leg was in and hated the fact this nurse was getting away with it. Without thinking of the consequences, she jumped up off her chair and held the nurse against the wall by her throat. The doctor was screaming at Bridie to let go, but she was so incensed she couldn't, convinced she was being accused of neglecting her own son.

Bridie was screaming that the woman wasn't fit to call herself a nurse, while the stubborn nurse continued to deny that she was the one who had taken Michael's stitches out. The doctor could see Bridie was fit to burst and quickly got the file out, which clearly showed that the nurse had indeed been the one who had treated him. Bridie couldn't keep the smirk off of her face. It wasn't just that she had been proven right, but she simply couldn't stand lies and would have been far more understanding if the nurse had simply admitted her mistake. Needless to say, that particular nurse never treated young Michael again.

Mick and Michael became increasingly inseparable, with the little boy mimicking his daddy wherever he went. Perhaps inspired by his time at the hospital, Michael particularly loved playing at being a doctor, complete with toy medical kit and plastic stethoscope. He loved nothing more than listening to Mick and Bridie's hearts, shaking his head and then announcing that they were dying.

On one occasion Mick groaned and asked if there was any way he could be saved. Michael said he could probably be spared if he rolled up his sleeve and had an injection. Playing along, Mick rolled it up and looked away, grimacing in mock terror as he awaited the pretend nip. As a result, he didn't see Michael take out a long fisherman's needle and jab it right into his unsuspecting arm. Bridie only just managed to hold back her tears of laughter as Mick held back a few colourful words!

Christina was also a big part of their life at this time. Inseparable from her big cousin Michael, she remembers her Aunty Bridie being a major influence during her childhood. She fondly recalls them all gathering at her granny's house to eat meals together. Even as a youngster she was impressed by her Aunty Bunty's immaculate style and elegance. Bridie was able to do everything: fixing the food, looking after the kids and always being easy to talk to. Fun to be around, Christina knew Bridie was there for her whenever she needed her.

Bridie fell pregnant with a much longed-for second child when Michael was two. She was ecstatic and Mick was also over the moon. They loved being parents and couldn't wait to have a little brother or sister for Michael. Bridie knew they would love this child as much as they adored their precious firstborn and couldn't wait to hold a baby in her arms again. She knew her family would be on hand to support her as always, and it was an exciting time as they made plans for the future. Mick was like the cat that had got the proverbial cream as he looked forward to becoming a dad again. The whole family was delighted for them and life couldn't have been better for the young McGoldrick family.

Sadly, it wasn't to be, and Bridie suffered a devastating miscarriage. Their hearts were broken as they were left to imagine what could have been, and Bridie's heart ached at the loss. She and Mick didn't understand why it had happened, but eventually decided to try again. Bridie fell pregnant five times, but despite remaining hopeful each pregnancy resulted in miscarriage, and at the age of thirty-two she stopped conceiving. The couple tried to put it behind them and move on, happy to have been blessed with Michael, but both felt brokenhearted over their loss.

Michael blossomed into a happy, healthy little boy, who was extremely sociable and always full of fun. He started school at five and charmed the teachers just as much as he had his own family. He didn't get off to the best start, though, as he heard the bell for playtime on the first day and assumed he could go home, promptly walking out of the school gates to return to his mum, figuring his work for the day was done. He was eventually persuaded to return and informed that he would have to stick it out every weekday thereafter!

The McGoldrick house was always noisy as young Michael delighted in telling stories and playing games, and both parents were only too happy to join in. Bridie kept up their Catholic traditions, so young Michael would accompany his parents to weekly Mass, just as she had with her own parents. Young Michael hadn't quite grasped the meaning of the word 'silence', and on one occasion he nearly brought the roof down with his loud commentary.

There was a giant crucifix at the back of the chapel with a wonderful carving of Jesus on it. At Consecration, while the congregation was sitting in complete silence, Michael piped up with, "Mammy, Mammy! You never told me Jesus wore a nappy!" Bridie nearly fell off her chair with embarrassment. It seemed the fun and forthrightness Bridie and Mick had in common was rubbing off on their son. And it wasn't only the McGoldricks who were affected by Michael's observation. The priest told Bridie as she was leaving chapel that he had barely been able to stifle his laughter at the remark and would never be able to look at that crucifix the same way again!

Just as she was beginning to feel as though her life was back on track and she was happy again, with her loving husband and beloved boy by her side, and surrounded by her precious family, an unforeseen bombshell shocked Bridie to the core. The three of them had booked a Butlin's holiday in Ayr, and everyone was really looking forward to it, especially Michael. A week before they were due to go, Bridie answered the phone to hear Margaret screaming, "Our Pat is dead! Our Pat is dead!" Bridie was completely shocked and couldn't process her sister's words. Her darling brother Pat was only twenty-nine but had died of a heart attack, and Bridie was utterly devastated.

Arrangements were made for Bridie, Mick and Joe to see to the funeral details down in London, where Pat had been living, as John and Christine were in no fit state to go. The trio set off in the car to collect his body, and on the way there the fan belt broke, so Bridie took her tights off so they could be used to repair it. Under normal circumstances she would have laughed, but she simply sat on the grass verge at the side of the road breaking her heart, still unable to accept that Pat was dead.

Bridie also felt great sorrow for her sister. Margaret was completely devastated, as she had been like a mother hen to Pat, always looking out for him when they were young. She had always adored him, and he had thought she was brilliant in return. They had enjoyed such a close bond, and the fact that Pat had moved away from Glasgow had done nothing to damage it.

When they arrived in London, Mick and Bridie had the grim task of ensuring Pat's body was prepared for the burial back in Scotland. Bridie's resourcefulness came in handy even at this tragic time. She went to the undertaker's at Francis Chapel, where his body lay. The parlour had dressed Pat, but she saw a spot of blood on his body and knew Christine would also see it, so a quick-thinking Bridie placed a Mass card strategically over the mark to make sure her grieving mum wouldn't notice it. Bridie and John also spotted a label with Pat's name on tied around his toe. Bridie pulled it off so her parents wouldn't see it, saying that Pat wouldn't need it as God knew exactly who he was. She had no doubt that Pat had gone to be with the Lord in heaven, and that he was in a much better place. It was just far too soon for them all to get their heads around it.

It was a harrowing time for the family without the added problem of having the body transported home by train, which was exceptionally expensive, despite Pat having worked for the rail network. Thankfully, the undertaker became aware of their plight and advised them that flying the body home would be more affordable. Sad but grateful, the trio made the long journey home.

The family gathered at their parents' house, and the shocking loss impacted each of them deeply. Bridie was more grateful than ever for her little family, realising just how precious life was. Pat had died on the 3rd of July, 1973, and was buried on the 11th. While Bridie didn't know it at the time, July was to become an even more sorrowful month some years down the line.

All the sadness of this time had left Michael feeling desperate for his holiday. He pestered Bridie constantly, pleading to go away to Butlin's as originally planned before Pat's death. John and Christine insisted the couple take the youngster away, telling Bridie they would be fine and trying to cope with their grief as best they could. She reluctantly agreed, knowing how excited her son was at the prospect of a trip to Ayr.

Just before they set off, Bridie was in the kitchen making custard for her parents in a bid to entice them to eat, as they were both too grief-stricken to care about themselves. Michael had gone outside to play and she was stirring the pot when there was a knock at the door and in walked a policeman. Bridie just stood there, stirring away, as he asked whether or not she had a little boy. When she answered yes, he told her to come with him as there had been an accident. Instantly in shock, Bridie kept stirring away at the custard, unable to respond.

She quickly snapped out of it and ran outside, screaming, to find Michael. A crowd had gathered around Michael, who was lying on the ground unconscious, having suffered a bad fall. The policeman barred Bridie's way, advising her to go and get Mick. Bridie was so hysterical the policeman felt it necessary to slap her face to calm her down before driving her to Mick's work. Mick collapsed as soon as he was told Michael was being taken to hospital. After the trauma of Pat's death, Bridie was unable to process what was happening and could only watch in horror as events unfolded.

CHAPTER 9:
Bedside Manners

Michael had been playing with his friends and had suffered a nasty fall. He was taken to hospital, still unconscious, where it was discovered that he had broken his right arm and shattered the femur in his left leg, as well as having concussion. The doctor came out and told them Michael was to be transferred to intensive care for close observation because of the severity of the concussion. Bridie and Mick had to change into hospital gowns before they were allowed in to see him and were visibly shocked when they saw his right arm in a cast and his left leg in traction. It was devastating to see his body all battered and broken, and Bridie was so beside herself she had to be given a sedative. Michael, on the other hand, was in excellent spirits when he came round. The first question he asked was whether or not he they would be going on their holiday. Sadly, the answer was no!

Mick and Bridie stayed with Michael until he fell asleep that night, but were advised to go home and get some rest as the road to recovery was likely to be a long one. They reluctantly agreed. The priest was waiting to see them when they arrived home. He was a regular visitor to Bridie's parents' home, as by this time Christine was suffering badly with arthritis and John was nearly blind. Uncharacteristically, Bridie was not in the mood to be polite or respectful. The priest thought it would be a good idea to say a wee prayer, but the bold Bridie told him to get stuffed! With her brother dead and her little boy in hospital she was really angry with God, and she wasn't in the mood to sit around praying to him. The priest didn't argue with her; he just quietly left the house and allowed the couple some time to rest.

Michael rallied during the days and weeks that followed, despite being in great pain. He also struggled with practical tasks, such as going to the toilet and feeding himself. One mealtime he was trying to cut up his dinner with one hand and everything was sliding all over the place. Feeling exasperated, he complained about the greasy meat and potatoes he had been given. The nurse attending him took the plate away and called Michael a spoiled brat.

Once again, Bridie was absolutely incensed when she heard about this. Mick was unable to stop her as she marched down to the nurses' room and demanded to know who had called her boy a brat. Everyone fell silent and looked down at the floor. The surgeon appeared and told Bridie it wasn't a good idea to pursue the issue, but she refused to be swayed. She just stood there, raging and refusing to budge until the nurse who had done it eventually came out, crying and apologising. Bridie told her in no uncertain terms how awful she was for slandering her son, who was unable to cut up his food or sit himself up. The nurse said she hadn't been aware of his needs and hadn't noticed him struggling, but Bridie wasn't buying that. The angry mother told the nurse there was no way she would be going near her boy again. Sensing the depth of Bridie's disgust, the staff decided it would be best to move Michael to a smaller, more private ward. However, a wise sister decided he was going nowhere, and the nurse who had insulted him had a major change of heart and came to love and care for Michael well.

So, with a patient called Eddie on one side and another named Tommy on the other, Michael's long road to recovery began. Bridie was at the hospital for breakfast every morning and only left once he had fallen asleep at night. She washed and dressed him every morning and spent the entire day looking after her beloved boy. Michael quickly grew to enjoy all the attention and concern, though he started to go a bit stir crazy after a few days on the ward. It was really difficult being stuck in bed with no chance to run around or play with children of his own age, but Eddie and Tommy were brilliant and loved the entertainment the little chatterbox provided. He had a steady stream of visitors, and the room was full of toys to keep him entertained. Michael was still gutted he had missed his holiday, but Mick and Bridie were just relieved he had started to recover.

Their life at the hospital soon fell into a familiar pattern, and Bridie got to know every patient on the ward, along with their families. They all took Michael to their hearts, and the little boy continued to have a big impact on everyone around him. Michael was a keen Celtic supporter, and after a fellow patient had a chance meeting with then Celtic manager Jock Stein and mentioned Michael, two players were sent up to the hospital by Stein to visit him. Michael was absolutely speechless and just sat there, open-mouthed and giddy with delight.

There was one issue the little boy was struggling with, which he eventually confided to his mum. He had nothing on his bottom half because his left leg was still in traction, and he found this really embarrassing when he had to use the bedpan. The ever-resourceful Bridie grabbed a pair of his pyjamas, and, with a bit of creative sewing, managed to make a pair that covered his privates. Lo and behold, the wives of all the other men on the ward thought this was a brilliant idea, and pretty soon Bridie had the whole ward covered up!

The ward was a happy place, despite the patients' pain, and Bridie was always at the heart of it. Whether she was sewing up pyjamas or tackling issues on someone else's behalf, her strong desire to see people treated well ensured that she made her mark as much as Michael did. Mick came to the hospital every day after work and the rest of the family visited frequently. It was a testing time for them all, but they came through it as resilient as ever.

Bridie was constantly asking the staff to hurry up and let her son come home, but Michael's surgeon explained that the break in Michael's femur was one of the worst they had ever seen, and that he wanted to give the little boy the best possible chance of recovery. He asked Bridie to be patient and let him keep Michael in hospital while the femur healed rather than putting a pin in. She felt very torn, as it seemed as though he had been in hospital for so long, but the thought of her son having a limp and ending up with one leg shorter than the other horrified her. It was hard not having him at home, but she and Mick agreed to let the surgeon move slowly, and they were eventually rewarded when the surgery proved to be successful.

As ever, Mick was Bridie's tower of strength during this time, and their marriage grew in love and laughter as they dealt with all that was thrown at them. Michael was released from hospital after eight long weeks, having promised to look after himself at home. He was such a lively boy, and he really struggled with being cooped up, but his parents were delighted to have him home. They made all his favourite meals and bought him enough toys, books, sweets and comics to open his own little shop. It was all worth it to Bridie and Mick just to see him smile. The house was always busy with a steady stream of visitors, and Michael's friends and cousins were often fed and watered alongside him. The young family might not have had much, but they lived in a sharing community. No one was ever turned away at teatime; the McGoldricks just made whatever they were having stretch a little.

Sometimes during his recovery period Bridie believed her son was simply enjoying the fresh air outside John and Christine's living room window, when in reality he was playing football on his crutches! It was years before she found out that her impatient patient had ignored her instructions, but it didn't come as a huge surprise. Christina was partly responsible for leading her cousin astray. Being the only girl in the family she got away with a great deal and certainly used it to her advantage. Even from a young age Michael was a sweet, gentle boy, and Christina loved being around him, especially as he was so protective of her. The family twigged that she wasn't quite as innocent as her butter-wouldn't-melt look suggested, and cottoned on to the fact that she was the instigator of a fair bit of trouble. However, this did nothing to stop her remaining as close to young Michael as their mothers had been as girls. History was certainly repeated itself as the younger, more boisterous Christina got the older, softer Michael into all sorts of scrapes.

Football had always been important to Michael, and there was a very important ritual that took place every night in the McGoldrick household once he was fully recovered. When Mick arrived home from work he would take Michael outside to play football with him, come rain or shine. They loved playing together, and Mick was so happy spending time with his boy. Even before he had eaten his dinner he would be out there, running around.

Bridie soon made peace with God again, despite her anger following Pat's early death and Michael's accident. Together with her husband and son she was a regular at the local chapel. Michael had an insatiable appetite for knowledge and was always ready to ask a thousand questions. On one occasion he wanted to know why, since Jesus had died on the cross, they took up a collection for him, as he surely wouldn't need any money in heaven. When it was explained that the collection went to poor children in Africa who had nothing, he put his hand in his pocket and brought out the money he had saved for sweets, declaring that they needed it more than he did, as he had a nice home and plenty to eat. A man who had been standing behind them and heard everything leaned over and gave Michael some money, saying it was the nicest gesture he had seen in a long time. Michael was chuffed, and not for the first time Mick and Bridie beamed with pride at the kind heart of their little boy.

Bridie continued to live as she always had, looking out for those who mattered most to her. Her parents were rapidly ageing, and her beloved father was completely blind by this point. No longer able to light his own pipe, Bridie would light it for him and help out wherever she could, but she found it hard to take as he became increasingly confused and frail. Seeing him deteriorate was so sad, especially as he had always been her hero. One frequent visitor to the McGeown house was a local nun who brought John the same present every time: a packet of tobacco for his pipe. It wasn't the Condor brand John loved, but the family always accepted it thankfully, and as the local shop loved the family so much its owners would swap the tobacco for his favourite brand afterwards.

Bridie was there, holding her father's hand, right to the end. One day he simply took his hand out of hers and quietly blessed himself before silently succumbing to pneumonia. Her daddy was gone, and despite being a happily married woman with a child of her own, she was devastated, knowing she would miss the feeling of protection he gave her terribly. Although she understood that it was a natural part of life, Bridie wasn't prepared for the shock of his passing. As usual, Mick was her rock. He always seemed to know what to say and do to keep her going. Bridie thanked God for her blessings once again, as she was so grateful to have Mick and her family around her. Michael was only nine at this point, yet despite his youth he had a good understanding of the circle of life. He took his mother's hand one day and said something that rendered her speechless: "Mammy, I know it's really sad, but it was worse when Uncle Pat died because he never got so long on this earth."

The family turned out in force to say goodbye to the beloved husband, father and grandfather who had loved and provided for them all their lives. Two priests led the service in a packed chapel, and, though absolutely mortified, Bridie was delighted by the turnout and by the widespread admiration for her father. One of the priests told Bridie he had never met anyone so destined for heaven, as John had been such a faithful, God-fearing man. He also said John was the most honest man he had ever met. One time while he was cleaning the boiler in the chapel John had found a substantial amount of money that had been dropped or lost over the years. He had gathered it up in bags and handed it over to the priest. The priest had wanted to share some of it with John, but he wouldn't take a penny, even though they probably could have done with the money at home. Bridie was so proud that other people recognised the fact her dad would never have done anything corrupt or underhand.

The death of her husband prompted the decline of Bridie's beloved mother. Christine quickly went from being the happy matriarch to a shadow of her former self. She was absolutely devastated by the passing of her soulmate. They had shared everything and had always been together, never failing to be there for their kids. It broke Bridie's heart to see her mother suffer so terribly with her grief. Christine was struggling with an initially undiagnosed illness and was taken into hospital at the age of seventy-seven, and Bridie could see that she was fading away.

Realising she was not being treated well on the ward, Bridie demanded she be brought home. The horrible decline into Alzheimer's had begun and it was harrowing for the family to watch. Christine rapidly changed from the mummy Bridie had known and loved, as the cruel disease ravaged her mind and body. Concerned about leaving Christine on her own, Mick and Bridie moved her into their home so they could look after her properly. She had moments of lucidity, but while she retained a great memory for events that had happened years earlier, she had no short-term memory at all and struggled with living in the present.

It was a sad but busy time for Bridie, as Uncle Mick and Aunty Lizzie (who had brought Mick up) had come over to visit from Northern Ireland and decided to stay. The house was rather crowded, with Christine sleeping on an airbed and Uncle Mick and Aunty Lizzie set up in another room. Bridie's brother Joe was having problems with his two boys, so Bridie and Mick had offered to take in his youngest, Jonny, for a while. He was fourteen at the time, so twelve-year-old Michael was happy to share his bedroom, while Mick and Bridie slept on a single mattress in the living room.

It was cramped and a bit difficult, but they made it work, with plenty of time for laughter in amongst the sadness. Not everyone was full of integrity and fairness, however, as Uncle Mick was very demanding. Every morning he ate seven Weetabix followed by about ten slices of toast, and he would just sit there expecting Bridie to fetch it all for him. Mick didn't appreciate his uncle's behaviour but Bridie felt obligated because he was family. Sadly, after just six weeks of staying with them, Aunty Lizzie died unexpectedly, which came as a bitter blow. Still enjoying being waited on by Bridie, the overbearing Uncle Mick recognised he was on to a good thing with them and settled in for the long haul.

Meanwhile, Christine's health had deteriorated drastically, and she was no longer the polite, kind, gentle lady she had always been. She often swore and would call Bridie every name under the sun; names her dignified mother never would have used had she been in her right mind. Bridie nursed Christine around the clock and spent much of her time praying for the strength to get through each day. It was horrible to see her mother suffering, especially when it got to the stage when Christine no longer recognised her own daughter. It was also a frustrating time, as Bridie would take her to the toilet, clean her up, get her dressed and then lift her up to take her into the next room when Christine would need to go to the toilet again, and she wouldn't wait. Christine had always been such a lady – so well dressed and full of poise – and it was heartbreaking for the family to see her like this. The only blessing was that Christine wasn't aware of how she was behaving, as she would have been mortified by if she had.

Bridie endured sleepless nights, insults, mood swings and a whole host of other issues that often come with Alzheimer's, as well as the physical burden of caring for her mother. She had brought Christine home in January and nursed her right through until May. Then one Sunday evening she was watching television with Christine sitting on her knee, busily talking away to her mum. Bridie noticed Christine wasn't responding and presumed she was asleep, so she held her tightly, engrossed in her programme. After a short while Bridie sensed something was wrong and realised her mother had died in her lap. It was a mercifully peaceful end to such a turbulent time for the family.

The family was united in grief, and everybody rallied round to give Christine a great send-off. Once again, it was clearly apparent just how cherished the family was by the local community. Even though Christine had shouted and sworn at them during the latter stages of her life, her friends and the local nuns were all there to celebrate her life and mourn her passing.

The service was lovely, and Mick was Bridie's strong tower throughout. But even though they had enjoyed good, long lives, losing both her parents was almost too much for Bridie to bear. It suddenly dawned on her that they would never again be able to offer her advice, give guidance or even just be there to see Michael grow up. She felt completely gutted and exhausted by it all.

Frank had moved to Holland with his wife six years before Christine died and didn't make it home for the funeral. Even though it was far away and travel was expensive, Bridie was surprised he didn't return. With no internet back then, and money in short supply on both sides, they drifted apart. Although the siblings had once been inseparable, their lives had taken them in different directions.

Life had changed forever, and Bridie knew she would have to continue without her beloved parents. Although it was all part of the circle of life, it was the end of a wonderful chapter in the story of her life.

CHAPTER 10:
Left, It's All That's Right...

Bridie didn't have time to sit around mourning her mother for long, as Uncle Mick was still proving quite a handful and demanding attention all the time. He told them he had severe stress issues and wasn't able to use his voice. He only left his room to sit in a chair in the living room, and Mick had to bathe and shave him. Though she felt very sorry for him, Bridie was driven almost to distraction by the constant demands he made on her time.

Mick felt a little sceptical about their house guest and eventually told the family doctor all about it. The GP visited them at home and was livid when he saw the way Mick and Bridie were being abused. He threatened to have him taken away and confined in a hospital if he didn't stop this outrageous behaviour. Then the doctor took Mick and Bridie downstairs and told them there was absolutely nothing wrong with Uncle Mick. He was just being downright lazy.

Mick was raging. He threatened to toss Uncle Mick out and leave him to fend for himself if his behaviour didn't change, and it did change... for all of about three days! Bridie and Mick were no soft touches, but they had a sense duty that stopped them throwing him out. Although she knew he was playing games, Bridie's loyalty prevailed.

All the while, thirteen-year-old Michael was growing up to be a considerate, well-mannered young man who was loved by his peers as well as by his relatives. The community where they lived was as close-knit as ever, and young Michael soon learned the benefits of having a 'weel-kent' (popular) face. He was always willing to lend a hand to anyone in need, though he also enjoyed the rewards that came with carrying someone's shopping home or running to the shops for a neighbour. Michael was a wind-up merchant like his dad, and he never stood still except to give his mother a hug. His cousin Jonny was always by his side, and the pair would hide chocolate in their room and have midnight feasts. Bridie knew all about it, of course, but she was just glad they were happy and having fun, as both had seen a lot of heartache during their young lives.

Christina loved the fact that, although her cousin was growing up fast, he was still the kind, protective giant he had always been. Michael was the best person to have around, both in and out of the playground, and she relished their close relationship. He was polite and clever at school, and everybody loved him. It benefited Christina that her cousin was tall, handsome and the nicest guy around. He was also really protective of her, even though she often did things he ended up getting the blame for. The one flaw Christina knew of was his clumsiness. Even as a teenager he could trip over a match, and on several occasions she found herself doubled over in laughter as Michael lay in a heap having just stood up or walked into a room. He was as enthusiastic about life as he had been as a child, and probably just about as coordinated!

Although the McGoldrick house had been crowded, Bridie always enjoyed having family around her. With both parents gone, as well as Pat and Aunty Lizzie, she felt a real sense of loss and struggled to get over it. She didn't have much time for wallowing, however, as Uncle Mick had returned to his old ways and was being extremely demanding. She kept pandering to him because her sense of duty outweighed her frustration, but it wasn't easy.

The biggest ray of sunshine in Bridie and Mick's lives was all the fun there was to be had with their golden boy, who was still charming the birds off the trees as a teenager. Everyone knew and loved Michael McGoldrick, and throughout his teenage years Bridie never heard him utter a swear word. His language may have been different on the football field when his parents weren't around, but he was always polite and respectful in their company.

Given Bridie's love for home-making and hospitality, it was no surprise that the McGoldrick house was where Michael and his large group of friends usually hung out. The house was always filled with laughter, friendly pranks and testosterone, and Bridie loved it. She made many a sandwich and pot of homemade broth to feed them all. Although the violence of the city hadn't impacted her family, she was aware it existed and was glad to have her boy and his friends at home, where she knew they would be safe and relatively well behaved.

On one occasion Bridie and Mick found adult magazines in Michael's room. At first Bridie said nothing; she just handed them to her son and let him do the talking. Mick's nephew Martin was staying with them at the time, and their faces were a picture. Desperately embarrassed, the pair explained that the magazines belonged to another boy who had come to the house one night and left them there. They seemed as shocked as Bridie at the content, although they had more than likely sneaked a peek!

Mick and Bridie couldn't help laughing once they had left the room at the sheer embarrassment on the boys' faces. To make it even funnier, the boy they belonged to came to the house that night. Before he left, Bridie told him to hang on as she had his books, then she promptly handed him the magazines. His expression was one of absolute shock, as he didn't have a clue how to react. It took young Michael a while to live the episode down, and there was plenty of friendly banter about it around the house.

Michael continued to do well at school and always had excellent report cards. Mick and Bridie were so proud of how clever and genuinely nice their son was. He never really excelled at art and hated technical drawing, but was especially good at English, history and maths. Bridie never had to worry about what the future held for

Michael, as she felt confident that he would achieve whatever he set his mind to.

There was one time, however, when Michael felt as though he had blown it. He had gone away for a school trip when he was sixteen feeling really excited. He had promised to have fun and behave himself, and Mick and Bridie were pleased to see him enjoying a bit of independence. But when he came back on the Sunday he was quiet… Far too quiet.

They knew something was up, and sure enough Michael eventually told his parents that four pupils had been suspended for getting drunk. He added that they didn't need to worry as he wasn't one of them. The following day he was sent home from school, also suspended. Bridie listened patiently as he explained that because he was the biggest he had been the one to go and buy the drink for the others. He hadn't touched a drop himself, but hadn't liked to say no to his friends. Michael was livid about being suspended, as he couldn't understand what he had done wrong.

He was sick with worry; not about what the school might do, but about what his father would think when he told him. When Mick came home, Michael said, "Dad, I'm in trouble." Mick told him to explain the situation quietly and calmly, promising to help if he could. Realising his dad might be able to fix the problem, Michael relaxed a bit. Although he was annoyed at being unfairly suspended, in his opinion, he had been terrified that he wouldn't be able to take his O levels and that his future would be completely ruined.

Mick may have been understanding, but Bridie was in no mood to agree that he was innocent and had been treated harshly by his teachers. The next morning she marched him straight up to the school, explaining on the way that if one of the kids had been taken ill or committed a crime while under the influence he would have been responsible. She made it clear that the man in the shop could have lost his job as a result, and that Michael was simply paying the consequences for breaking the law.

It took a while for the penny to drop, as Michael had initially felt they should have been pleased he hadn't drunk anything himself, but he eventually recognised that what he had done was wrong. Because he had been such a good pupil up until then the school happily reinstated him, but not before he had been sick with fear and apologised to his parents a thousand times. Bridie and Mick naturally forgave this rare moment of madness, and they continued to share many happy moments as a family.

It wasn't all sunshine and roses, however, as times were tough for the family financially. There was widespread unemployment during the seventies, with high inflation and bleak conditions for many of the families around them, and Bridie and Mick needed a helping hand themselves on occasion. They were struggling at this particular time, as Mick worked at the Avon tyre factory and the staff were out on strike. Unbeknown to Bridie he had put some money on the horses with a couple of friends one Saturday, and between them they had won £3,600. Despite having to be split three ways, this was an absolute fortune at the time. He received the money on the Monday, then walked in and showered his speechless wife with the notes. It was an amazing surprise amid difficult circumstances. Mick still loved looking after Bridie, and was especially delighted to be able to surprise her when they were so desperate. The little family celebrated in style with special meals, new clothes, and gifts for Michael and the rest of the family.

Life never seemed to stay on an even keel for the McGoldricks, and it was around this time that Bridie had to leave her job at Carr's due to her arthritis. It had spread to her knees and hips by this point, leaving her with chronic pain she never recovered from. She reluctantly started using two sticks to help her get around. She was devastated to be so immobile, knowing poor health would plague her forever.

To make matters worse, she had to fight to get the sick pay she was entitled to. A staunch believer in social justice and human rights, she was disgusted to find that the system seemed to work against the poorest in society and those with the greatest needs. For someone who had worked so hard all her adult life, it was absolutely galling that the government wanted to keep her entitlement from her. When Mick and Bridie were incensed when they read about a family that was receiving money to visit their son in prison while Bridie was receiving sick pay to live on, and the pair began to dig deeper into the social security system.

Both were members of the Labour Party, so they went to visit their local MP, Jimmy Wray, where they found out everything they could about what Bridie was entitled to and how to apply for it. There was a wealth of information out there once they started to dig around. Jimmy Wray, a man in the Labour Party named Quentin Oliver who was also keen to see folks get what they were entitled to, and a couple of other folks proved to be a great support to the couple, and a lifelong interest in the benefits system began. There was a manual at the time known as The Yellow Book, which contained all the relevant information regarding benefits. The couple found it unfathomable that their local benefits office didn't have one, so they obtained a copy and got themselves well acquainted with the whole benefits system.

The local welfare rights advice van, provided by the council, became their second home, and the employees there soon came to recognise Bridie and Mick as people who knew what they were talking about. The pair were tenacious, arguing their case and refusing to be fobbed off by unhelpful officials. The needs in their community were great, but the government wasn't swift to point out what people were entitled to. The couple made sure there was nobody in their close community who didn't get some sort of government relief. Bridie was extremely effective, and was described as a 'firebrand' on more than one occasion as a result.

She also discovered that if residents had special needs they were entitled to additional funds to cover items such as extra underwear, bedding and laundry services for the incontinent. The law stated that people had to ask for these funds, but the Social Services staff knew ordinary people, and especially the elderly, were afraid to do so. Pretty soon there were more smiles and sighs of relief than tears of despair echoing through the close-knit Gorbals community as Bridie spread the news.

Not everyone who saw Bridie in action was impressed, however. One young man who had just started working at the Social Security office remarked during a meeting that if Bridie was fit enough to fight for people's rights she was surely fit enough for work. Bridie remained silent. She bided her time, waiting until the end of the meeting before sarcastically remarking that she owed him an apology as she hadn't congratulated him on becoming a doctor. He stared blankly at her, the penny finally dropping when Bridie also remarked that if he could just give her the new heart, lungs and hips her body needed she would go back to work immediately. He didn't have a word to say after that!

Mick shared Bridie's passion for justice and equality, and was very active in campaigning for the Birmingham Six and the Guildford Four, understanding the need to speak out against questionable convictions and obvious bigotry. In both cases, Catholic men of Northern Irish descent were found guilty of murder by planting bombs in pubs, with forced confessions used to convict them due to a complete lack of evidence. Campaigns ran for years to prove their innocence, and eventually their cases were brought back to court. Having spent years in prison their convictions were quashed, but not before their and their families' lives had been well and truly ruined.

As formidable a duo as Mick and Bridie were, there was one person who didn't quake in his boots at the sight of them, and that was young Michael. He respected and knew when they were angry or serious about something, but he always felt loved and secure. He also knew that his streetwise parents often sat and laughed at his antics when he went up to bed. He realised Mick was a soft touch most of the time, but always knew not to push him too far. Likewise, Christina recognised that Mick was the quieter, more softly spoken of two, but such was his presence that people always listened when he spoke. She often couldn't keep up when he was talking about important issues, but she knew it was worth listening to, and years later she realised Mick's was wise advice she could always rely on.

As for Bridie, her loveable son had her wrapped around his little finger from day one. Even when she was being firm with him, Michael would give her a great big hug and a kiss, then say, "Yes, but sure I'm a nice guy, amn't I, Mum?" And of course she had to agree that he was! Mick and Bridie made everything they did fun, and Christina enjoyed hanging around them all. They were still so in love, with hearts wide open to those around them and always ready to help out wherever they could.

One very important aspect of Bridie's early family life that she had carried over into her adult life was her faith. Although she wasn't in a close relationship with the Lord at this time, the McGoldricks were committed to going to Mass on a Saturday night and Sunday morning. God was the one they thanked, prayed to, believed in and even feared a little.

Three years after Christine's death, Mick's Uncle Mick passed away. Although he had been a difficult man to deal with – angry and bitter throughout his time with them, and running Bridie ragged for years – it was still a sad time. Given that family meant so much to Bridie, dealing with another death was painful, and it altered her world once again.

Bridie continued to see Margaret as often as possible, catching up on her sister's news during their regular get-togethers. Margaret was married by this time and had a second daughter named Karen with her new husband. She moved out of the Gorbals to nearby Govanhill, but that didn't stop the sisters from being as close as ever. Their children loved spending time together and the mums would do the usual sisterly things; seeing to each other's clothes, hair and make-up, and going to the pictures.

Mick had a fixed Saturday routine. He started off playing football with Michael, then had a few games of darts at the pub in the afternoon. In the evening, he, Bridie and Michael would get a Chinese takeaway or go out with friends. The first Friday of each month was date night. The couple didn't talk politics or family that night; they just had a laugh together and spent time enjoying each other's company. Nobody made Bridie's heart flutter like Mick McGoldrick, and his blue eyes never stopped making her go weak at the knees.

Their house was often the resource centre for neighbours who were desperate to find out what to apply for and how to go about it, so there was never a dull moment for the McGoldricks. Michael was well aware of all that his parents did for the neighbourhood, and the three of them cared deeply about human rights. They weren't interested in political point-scoring; all they knew was that every person deserved to have enough food, clothing, a roof over their head and money to live on, regardless of their social status.

But although they were heavily involved in the welfare rights of so many around them, and delighted to fight on their behalf, they were always happiest when they were alone together. Mick was so happy with his life that he had a permanent smile on his face. He made others laugh and was very often the comedian in the room. Michael was growing up to be very like his dad, and the pair of them were forever playing practical jokes on Bridie and winding her up. She certainly needed her wits and patience about her at all times. Despite being in constant pain and using sticks to get about, Bridie loved her busy life. But as full as it was, there was always room for one more…

CHAPTER 11:
Here We Go Again...

One summer during the eighties the McGoldricks travelled to Craigavon, County Armagh, to visit family for a few weeks, and it wasn't long before history seemed to be repeating itself. Twenty by this point, Michael was enjoying the freedom he had been given to hang out with his cousins and all their friends. He was also enjoying the attention of the local girls, who were all rather enamoured with the big, handsome Scottish guy. A few days in he met a girl called Sadie from Lurgan, and the pair instantly became inseparable. Sadie was the first girl to truly capture his heart, and Bridie could tell from very early on that Michael was in love. It was impossible not to reminisce about her own romance with Mick all those years before as she saw her son so caught up with his Irish sweetheart.

Michael began writing to Sadie on his return to Glasgow, but more often he would phone his soulmate, which meant that Mick and Bridie's bills went through the roof! Michael came in one night, just two weeks after his holiday, and said he had met up with Sadie, who had come over from Belfast for the day just to see him. The pair had enjoyed a few hours together in Glasgow city centre before she had to return home. Sadie was completely smitten with Michael, and he was head over heels for her.

They would visit each other whenever they had the time and money, but it was never enough, so it came as no great surprise when Michael gathered the families together, and, after giving Sadie a giant pink teddy bear, proposed in front of them all. She immediately said yes. It was a beautiful relationship, and Bridie was delighted to welcome Sadie into the family. She quickly became a welcome and much-loved addition to the McGoldrick clan.

Wedding preparations quickly began, and soon enough the pair were hitched at St Peter's chapel in Lurgan, with both sets of relatives there to celebrate the union, and Michael's cousin Martin as his best man. Bridie and Mick travelled over on the ferry with the Glasgow contingent, including Margaret's second daughter Karen, their local priest Father Tony and Aunty Marion, a neighbour who had regularly babysat Michael when he was a child.

The bride and groom made a stunning couple. Sadie looked like a beautiful little doll, while Michael was taller and more handsome than ever. Everyone had a great laugh at the reception, with plenty of dancing, jokes and banter. It was a wonderful wedding and a great opportunity for the McGoldrick side of the family to spend time with Mick, as they had barely seen each other since Mick moved to Glasgow.

Michal and his young bride lived in Dundonald for a while before moving back to Glasgow, where Michael started working towards a nursing qualification. He worked as a nurse at the Glasgow Victoria Infirmary, about ten miles from where he had grown up and the same hospital Christine had carried Bridie to on her back when Bridie had an abscess in her ear. Michael loved his job, and his caring nature was perfectly suited to looking after patients. His own lengthy stay in hospital as a young boy no doubt influenced his career choice, and he was determined to provide the same care and attention he had received. He loved every aspect of his work, and was especially good at putting people at ease before offering a listening ear and a helping hand. Sadly, he was a little too helpful. Despite the recommended advice not to, he was told to lift a patient from the bed one day.

Doing so gave Michael such a bad back injury that it forced him to give up nursing completely.

Sadie's own nursing skills came in handy around this time, as Bridie was in terrible pain and had to have her gall bladder removed. Her stomach had been giving her problems for years, and it had almost come as a relief when they found out what had been causing the pain. Sadie looked after her mother-in-law, tending to her needs and generally ensuring that Bridie made the best possible recovery after a fairly major operation.

It wasn't long before a delighted Michael and Sadie announced they were expecting a baby. Mick and Bridie were over the moon to hear this news, and Bridie was so excited she spoke to the baby every time she saw Sadie throughout the pregnancy. She knew she was going to adore this little bundle from the moment she found out they were expecting. Mick felt the same way, though his medical knowledge clearly hadn't improved much, as he thought that because Sadie was a nurse she might have some inside knowledge that would protect her from the pain!

Sadie had a normal labour, with the usual amount of pain included, and the young couple made it to the hospital just in time for the birth. Their little girl, Emma, was soon born, and another wonderful chapter in their lives began. She was absolutely perfect, with a full head of beautiful dark red hair.

Bridie took a lovely satin gown into the hospital and held Emma in her arms, savouring every little part of her. Although she had known for many months that she was going to be a grandmother, and had been extremely excited about it, she hadn't anticipated the feelings of love and protection that rose up in her on holding Emma for the first time. Emma was the most beautiful baby in the world to her doting grandmother, and Bridie knew this lovely little girl would always have a very special place in her heart.

Another hugely significant moment occurred that night when Michael picked his newborn daughter up and placed her in Mick's arms, declaring that he would try to raise her the way Mick had raised him. It was a very special moment for the whole family.

Sadie and Michael decided to have Emma baptised in Lurgan, where they were married, and once again a family trip over the Irish

Sea was arranged in celebration of the newest and prettiest McGoldrick. Bridie and Mick were joined by Mick's family and Sadie's relatives as they toasted the beautiful Emma. Bridie loved seeing her boy beaming with pride as his precious princess was baptised into the church family.

Sadly for Bridie and Mick, Michael and Sadie decided to return to Northern Ireland for good when Emma was just six months old. Although they were distraught to see them move away, they hoped the young family would have a better life there. Bridie knew she would miss them all, and particularly Emma, dreadfully.

She didn't have to miss them for long, though. A few months later, just days before her next birthday, Michael rang to ask what she wanted as a gift. "Our Emma, all wrapped up and put on the plane," Bridie joked. Michael told her to expect a delivery and kept checking she would be in on the morning of her birthday. Sure enough, when the day arrived they burst through the door to surprise her, placing Emma in her open arms. Emma had grown significantly since they had last seen her and Bridie and Mick couldn't get enough cuddles. They were also delighted to see their big boy and Sadie, and the five of them had a wonderful time together. It was clear that Michael and Sadie were enjoying life in Northern Ireland, but Michael always loved seeing the familiar sights of his beloved Glasgow.

It was heartbreaking having to say goodbye to them again when their time was up, and Bridie and Mick could hardly bear to stand and watch them drive away. Life felt so empty without the three of them around. Nevertheless, Bridie found herself needed by other relatives who had fallen on hard times. Her nephew and his wife had sadly split up, and he had completely walked away, leaving five young children without a father figure in an already tough economic climate.

Mick and Bridie didn't want to interfere, but they saw that the newly single mother was struggling to cope. Given how much they loved kids and helping those in need, they set about doing everything they could to support the young family. They gave her a hand with the housework and the kids' schoolwork. They helped the mother find affordable furniture and taught the kids how to look after their belongings. They also made sure they had school uniforms, play clothes and food in the cupboards.

Mick often took the boys out to play football, down to the park or to the shop for sweets, trying to make sure they knew that they were safe and loved. While they were out, Bridie would spend time with the mother, who was feeling a bit lost and overwhelmed. Bridie was always there to support and encourage, teaching her how to make soups and simple meals. The family flourished, and it was wonderful for Mick and Bridie to see them settled and happy.

The children responded well to this inpouring of love and it soon began to show in their schoolwork, with all five growing in confidence. One night the eldest boy relayed that his teacher said she had seen a massive improvement in his attitude, hygiene and work, and that she thought he was a very good and handsome pupil. His smile alone made everything they had done feel worthwhile for the kind-hearted McGoldricks. The kids were obviously grateful, but Bridie made sure they knew it was really their mum they should be thanking. She told them she and Mick were merely helping out, and that all credit must go to the mother, whose gratitude for the considerate couple went through the roof.

Bridie cared for the children the way she had cared for Michael: firmly but fairly. They all knew that her yes meant yes and her no meant no. Eventually the young mum found her feet and was able to look after the five children herself, especially as they were a largely well-behaved, considerate, easily managed bunch by that point. This was good timing, as Bridie needed to turn her attention to her own household. Having served his country and worked hard all his life, Mick was battling serious back pain. There was a problem with his discs, which left him in constant agony.

At the age of forty-eight it looked as though he would have to retire, but he wasn't prepared to go without a fight. Mick hated the idea of receiving sick pay and being forced to stop working, but after a spirited attempt to delay it, he was forced to take his leave. He was given a lump sum as he waved goodbye to the workforce. It initially felt as though he was skiving, and for a long time he couldn't accept that his days in regular employment were over.

This development caused the pair to reflect on their lot in life. Both in their late forties, and with no jobs to hold them back, there was only one place they wanted to be. Although they would miss their friends and family in Glasgow, they had helped many people stand on their own two feet and given others hope in their bleakest times. It was time to think about what they wanted to do, and they were both certain that they wanted to move closer to Michael, Sadie and Emma. In typical Bridie fashion, they decided to make the move to Ireland on the Tuesday after Mick finished work, and by the Sunday they were on the plane, knowing it was absolutely the right decision for them. They said their goodbyes to Glasgow, packed up all their belongings and moved in with Mick's sister Anna in Portadown.

Emma was fourteen months old by this time, so they wanted to be around to see her grow up, and they also felt it was important to spend more time with Mick's family. Moving to Northern Ireland would mean that his relatives could spend time with their family and share in their life. Bridie also had many relatives nearby, so they were never short of people to visit. Michael and Sadie were delighted, as they had missed the couple a great deal. Being close to her beloved boy and his family was such a blessing for Bridie, and they quickly settled in, almost feeling as though they had come home. All sorts of memories came flooding back as they visited their old childhood haunts, and the couple became like teenagers again as they visited their honeymoon destination and other places of romantic interest.

After living with Anna for three months they found a house near Michael's, which just happened to be right next door to Mick's elder brother Jim and his wife Maura. It was like another mini homecoming, and they quickly began to feel well and truly rooted in the Craigavon community. The couple bought a caravan in Warrenpoint and would often go up there for romantic breaks. Bridie couldn't have known when they first visited Warrenpoint during their honeymoon that they would be practising something they would love doing for the rest of their lives. Sex never lost its appeal within their happy marriage.

When they weren't heading down there for some intimate time alone, they would take some of the children from their extended families to give the parents a well-earned break. One family member who was particularly delighted to welcome them to Northern Ireland was Jaqueline McGoldrick, who was married to Mick's nephew and Michael's best man, Martin. Jacqueline was over the moon when

Bridie and Mick joined them, especially as she was also Scottish and had grown close to the couple while she was living in Glasgow.

This friendship remains close today. Always a welcome visitor, Jacqueline has journeyed through the many highs and lows of Bridie's life, and the McGoldricks' house has always felt like a second home to her. Mick and Bridie also became trusted confidantes for Jacqueline. She could tell them both anything, and they always had time for her. Bridie and Mick were also wonderful with Martin and Jacqueline's children, who still refer to them as Aunty Bridie and Uncle Mick.

Surrounded by her Irish family and friends, and being able to escape to Warrenpoint with her sweetheart whenever they felt like it, Bridie was truly in her element. The stunning beauty of Warrenpoint never failed to take her breath away, and she was constantly in awe of the spectacular mountains of Mourne, which tower above it like majestic warriors. There was no place on earth she would rather have been.

Bridie and Mick were both lovers of the simple life and a bit of tranquillity, but they usually had a full caravan. They loved being able to go away with Michael, Sadie and Emma or with Jaqueline's boys, Martin, Michael and Niall. In the summer holidays they would go from Monday to Friday and come home in time for the weekend. Not only were the parents grateful for the breather from their noisy offspring, but the kids were delighted, and all still have fond memories of these trips away. Sometimes it was just the brothers and other times they took their cousins with them, but whatever the combination it was always a good laugh. Uncle Mick would take the kids to the little patch of grass on the caravan site and play football with them for hours, then Aunty Bridie would shout them in for one of the amazing dinners she had prepared, which were perfect for the hungry little adventurers after a day in the great outdoors.

Bridie was always very generous with the boys, but try as they might they could never get her to spoil them with too many sweeties. There were great jars full of them in the caravan, and most of the other kids on the site liked to be in or around their van for this reason, but Bridie remained firm and fair whenever it came to dishing them out. Looking back, Jacqueline's oldest boy Martin realises how incredibly generous she was and how many sweeties he was given, but at the time he always wanted just one more!

Her formative years may have been spent on the streets of Glasgow, but Bridie's heart responded best to the beauty of nature. Spending time in this picturesque hideaway also encouraged her to spend time with her creator. It was hard not to think about her faith and the greatness of God when faced with his handiwork. But while Bridie's faith was an integral part of her life, it was still based on a fear of God rather than a relationship with him.

CHAPTER 12:
If You're Irish, Come In To The Parlour

The happy couple loved their new life from the off, and their house soon became a hub for the many family members, friends and neighbours who came to visit. It was especially delightful for Mick to enjoy this time with his relatives, and to see his son become a great father with a happy family of his own. Bridie had enjoyed a happy childhood, but her husband hadn't been so fortunate. It made her incredibly proud to see how considerate and caring a husband and father he was given how little love he had experienced growing up.

The couple quickly settled into the parish of St Anthony's. The local priest, Father Martin, was quite struck with the pair. He assumed they were celebrating an anniversary the first time he saw them as they were sitting so close in the pew and holding hands, but as the weeks passed by he realised they were just a couple of lovebirds who had never changed. Bridie felt a little embarrassed when she realised the priest could see them being so demonstrative from the altar… though never quite embarrassed enough to do otherwise!

The culinary delights of Ireland weren't lost on Bridie, who loved freshly baked soda bread, especially when it was served hot with a layer of butter so thick it looked like cheese. However, there were a few Scottish delicacies she just couldn't do without, such as crispy morning rolls and Scotch pies. Whenever any of her relatives came over from Glasgow she would ask them to bring some over.

Christina recalls every trip she made across the water being great fun. Bridie's niece wasn't only enamoured with the great hospitality, but also with all the laughter they shared. She adored her aunt's sense of adventure but also her calmness and compassion. Christina noticed that Bridie never raised her voice or resorted to bad language. She always kept a cool head in a crisis and had a kind word for everybody she saw.

Michael, Sadie and Emma came to visit once a week, and every Wednesday Bridie and Mick looked after Emma. They always looked forward to seeing their beautiful granddaughter with her infectious laugh and joyous nature. Every week Bridie was reminded what a kind and doting father her son was, and it made her immensely proud.

Life soon settled into a happy routine. On weekdays they watched Martin, Michael and baby Niall for Jaqueline and Martin, with Emma also in tow on Wednesdays. Emma was a happy, inquisitive child and Bride spent hours telling stories, singing songs and playing hide and seek with her. Mick was just as enthralled with his little granddaughter and never tired of letting her boss him around the house as she played her games. The whole family doted on her. Michael and Sadie often popped in for a visit as well, which delighted Bridie, who was desperate to maintain the close bond she had with her only child and his lovely wife. She needn't have worried, as Sadie also enjoyed their company and the five had many great laughs in their Craigavon house over the years. Sadie also had a beautiful singing voice, which Bridie loved to hear at family gatherings.

Everyone in the street knew they could come to the McGoldricks for a chat, a favour or some decent home cooking, and Bridie felt as though their life was finally complete. Mick disagreed, however! About a year after buying their house in County Armagh he came home with a little bundle of white fluff in his arms. A dog! This wasn't something Bridie had wanted or expected, but Mick charmed her into it, explaining the puppy was the runt of the litter and would have been put down if he hadn't taken her. Bridie still wasn't convinced, but the wee dog followed her everywhere, obviously sensing which side her bread would be buttered on. They named her Snowy, and she very quickly became a fully-fledged member of the McGoldrick family. Mick was so good with her, walking her for miles every day, and the couple embraced this new furry addition with their usual sense of fun and love.

Mick built Snowy an outdoor kennel, but was so concerned she wouldn't be comfortable he put carpets and a light inside. Bridie joked that the neighbours' dogs must have had kennel envy! She was a pampered pooch, enjoying a fried breakfast every morning and a hearty dinner with Mick and Bridie in the evenings. Not bad for the runt of the litter, but then Mick and Bridie had never been able to resist the underdog.

Jacqueline's boys couldn't wait to get round to the McGoldricks' home each morning and happily ran into the house. They were desperate to see what Aunty Bridie and Uncle Mick had in store for them, as there was always some sort of adventure to be had. Martin has particularly fond memories of the time they spent together. He particularly enjoyed the times just before and after school, when there was lots of bustle and busyness as the boys were fed and watered. Martin clearly had the McGoldrick line in patter, as he recalls being late one day and Mick trying to get them all ushered in, pointing out the time, to which Martin replied that it was his uncle's fault as Mick had given him two slices of toast instead of one that morning!

Saturday night was always curry night for the McGoldricks. Mick and Bridie would settle down with trays on their laps, along with their neighbour Alice and Snowy the dog, and the usual storytelling and laughter was never far away. Sunday nights would either be spent at a pub with Jim and Maura, driving to the seaside and enjoying a meal out, or spending time at other people's homes.

Michael often popped over on his way home from work, usually entertaining them with tales of his wee superstar, Emma. He was a great husband and dad, and everything he did was for the two lovely girls in his life. He was almost always saving up for something.

Ever since he was a child he had been in the habit of setting money aside for a rainy day, so Bridie had never worried about him that way. If he ever found himself a bit short as a child he would never ask for anything; he would just give a wee sigh, sit down beside his dad and then leave the room. Then Mick would follow his son out and give him a little something.

One time Mick came into the kitchen and said that he thought Michael needed money as he had given him the sigh routine. Bridie wasn't convinced but said they would need to give it to Michael and Sadie together, as she didn't want to give him anything without Sadie feeling included. Mick said she was a "wise wee wummin", a phrase he used frequently and with great admiration over the years. However, as Michael was leaving that night he put his hand in his pocket, and with a big smile gave the money he found there back to his father.

"There you go, Dad," he said. "I just wanted to know if that would still work!" Mick sat there, open-mouthed, as if to say, "You just played me!" Bridie still laughs at this story, delighted by the fact she had the measure of both father and son.

Bridie has always loved all the excitement of Christmas, and was in her element in those years after she moved to Craigavon. She and Mick would go to Michael and Sadie's on Christmas Day to enjoy the festivities, watch Emma unwrap her presents and enjoy a big Christmas dinner, then on Boxing Day the dinner would be at theirs. It was always the same: massive grilled T-bone steaks. They were a firm favourite with both Mick and Michael, and the various kids who came over would be given more presents and treats. They always gave their main presents on Christmas Day, and on Boxing Day wrapped up little things like oranges, socks, pencils, shampoo and silly toys. Then they would play games and eat lots, and of course Snowy was always included in the festivities!

Living in Northern Ireland didn't put an end to Bridie's close relationship with her sister Margaret or her brother John, who were both regular visitors to her home. She loved it when they came over, particularly when they brought the obligatory rolls and pies with them. John had been born in Ireland and felt a special affinity to the country. As boys, Michael and Martin had loved playing with Uncle John, so it was nice for Bridie to see him down on the floor tickling or arm-wrestling with their kids, especially as he had no children of his own. Everyone loved it when he came over, and John enjoyed the serenity of the caravan.

Margaret and Bridie always picked up where they had left off the previous time, talking for hours and putting the world to rights. The pair loved shopping together and hanging out. It reminded Bridie of their childhood, and she often wished their parents were with them to enjoy these happy times. It was important to Mick and Bridie that they continued to provide the level of care for others that John and Christine had offered, and to create a loving home with open doors. Thankfully, their marriage had always been a happy one, and even though they spent every day together Bridie still couldn't get enough of her man. He was the love of her life and her closest friend.

CHAPTER 13:
That's My Boy

Bridie's arthritis had worsened, and she was in terrible pain most of the time. She never went anywhere without her sticks, but she didn't let ill health stop her. The McGoldrick home was still a gathering point for the whole family, and it was rarely empty.

Bridie cherished every moment she spent with Michael, Sadie and Emma. Emma was a little doll and the apple of her daddy's eye. They looked so comical together: Michael at about six foot three and his wee girl up on his shoulders or holding his hand tightly. She had him wrapped around her little finger, and everyone could see that she was the boss. She had the most beautiful copper-coloured hair, and Sadie always had her dressed immaculately. Bridie could never resist buying her granddaughter pretty bows, ribbons and dainty little handbags with matching shoes. Emma was great company and seemed happy whether she was with adults or children. There was no doubt that she was her daddy's princess, however.

At the age of twenty-seven, Michael decided he wanted to go to Queens University Belfast to study for a degree in history and politics before becoming a teacher. Michael had always been clever at school but hadn't always relished spending time on his own doing homework. He hadn't wanted to go to university at seventeen, opting to do nursing instead. The back injury had forced him to give that dream up, so it was especially pleasing to his mother that he had decided to return to education as a mature student. Despite Sadie working hard as a nurse, times would have been financially tight for the couple with only her wage coming in, so Michael started driving a taxi to earn a bit of extra cash. As ever, Bridie was as proud as punch of her boy and was happy he would be doing something he really enjoyed. With his natural gift of the gab, Bridie had no doubt he would do well in the classroom. Given his wonderful storytelling ability and Celtic passion, it seemed as though Michael McGoldrick was made to educate future generations.

His nephew Martin knew Michael had all the qualities a good teacher should have. He loved that wherever he was or whoever he was talking to, Michael McGoldrick was always engaged and interested. Martin loved being at the house or caravan at the same time as Michael, as he was so friendly and down to earth, and just like his Aunty Bridie and Uncle Mick he would do anything for anybody. He was really easy to talk to, yet people listened to him whenever he spoke. He was a great mixture of his mum and dad, and young Martin would have loved to have a teacher like Michael.

Not everything in the garden was rosy for Bridie's boy, however, as the couple soon had to face a heartache his mother completely understood. Sadie was told she couldn't have any more children, which came as a major blow to them both. The whole family was supportive of the young couple, but Bridie knew more than most how they felt, given that she and Mick had desperately wanted another child themselves. But she also knew that having one happy, healthy child was a great blessing, and everyone was besotted with their little girl, just as Bridie had been with her boy.

Life soon settled into a new routine, with Michael studying in Belfast and driving his taxi in Lurgan. Bridie loved the fact that her son was so excited about his future. One night he called them three or four times to check they were home, as he was heading out to see them. Bridie sensed their son was excited about something, but he wouldn't say why he was so keen to pop over. Michael, Sadie and Emma eventually appeared with big grins on their faces.

Bridie had just remarked to Mick that it wouldn't have surprised her if Sadie were pregnant. Mick said that although he had often been amazed by women and their intuition, he was certain she was wrong this time because it was completely impossible. Sure enough, Bridie's gut feeling was correct, and it turned out the delighted couple were to become parents for the second time in October-time, just months after Michael was due to graduate. It was a miracle and everyone was over the moon.

Emma was seven by this point, and had long outgrown the crib and pram Mick and Bridie had bought her when she was born. They had been perfectly happy for Sadie to give them away to someone in need when the couple were told they couldn't have any more children, but on hearing this happy news Mick said that they would happily buy the same gifts for the new little one.

Bridie was so pleased for Michael, as he had been so keen to have a little brother or sister for Emma. She was also delighted for Sadie, as she knew only too well the heartache of longing for another child and being told it would never happen. Although it hadn't happened for her and Mick, she was delighted for them and for little Emma.

In the early summer of 1996, Mick and Bridie had the three young McGoldrick boys, Martin, Michael and Niall up at the caravan with them. They returned home on the 4th of July, excitedly looking forward to Michael's graduation the next day. The house was a hive of activity and anticipation, and all the ladies went down to the hairdressers to get dolled up so they could look their best for the ceremony.

Much to Bridie's dismay, Michael came in on the Thursday night with his hair cut really short. He saw her face and said: "Don't worry, Mum, it'll grow back." Then he turned to his dad and said: "Looks like we're having a race to lose our hair, but I think you're winning." Quick as a flash, Mick said: "At least mine had the grace to hang around and go grey first!"

Michael fell to his hands and knees with laughter. The pair were constantly joking around, and Bridie found herself bursting with joy as she reflected on all that was to come for her growing family. She was convinced that life couldn't get any better, and was desperately looking forward to meeting the new baby. At that moment, however, she was full of anticipation for Michael's graduation.

The great day dawned and the whole family, including Sadie's mother Pauline, who lived close by, had gathered for the ceremony. Michael looked so smart in his suit and gown, and although she acknowledged that everyone had done well, Bridie was sure that her son was the most popular graduate, convinced that he received the loudest cheer from his fellow students as he went up to receive his degree. Another person on the stage that day who managed to raise a healthy cheer was none other than Mary McAleese, who later became President of Ireland. Michael may not have held lofty aspirations to run a country, but he was ready and determined as he completed his academic studies. Bridie could tell that her son was held in the highest regard by his friends, and she cried tears of joy and pride as he walked up onto the stage. He was so strong and handsome, and she was well aware of the sacrifices he and Sadie had made to get to this point. It was wonderful to see all that effort pay off.

After all the photographs and back-slapping had come to an end, the delighted family set off for an expensive meal in town and a night of celebration. Everyone was so happy and proud, and a brilliant time was had by all. They had the long summer ahead of them, and life was good. They spent the night laughing and swapping stories.

At one point Bridie said she was glad she had never lied to Michael and had always brought him up to tell the truth. He looked at her with the big eyes that always melted her heart and said that there were actually two lies that had impacted him to that day. Bridie was horrified, but remained adamant that she had never told him anything that wasn't true. "Really?" he said. "What about the tooth fairy? And what about that old fat guy with the red suit and the white beard?" Bridie burst out laughing, as did everyone else at the table.

Sadly, the evening couldn't last forever, and Bridie and Mick had planned on setting off back to the caravan after dinner. It was touch and go whether they would make it to Warrenpoint, as there had been a lot of terror that summer. There was fear and anger in the air as the Drumcree standoff – an annual protest against Orange Order marches through Portadown – played out, and there were road blocks and police checks everywhere.

Protestant marchers wanted to parade down the mainly Catholic and republican areas of Garvaghy Road, while the Catholic residents were vehemently against it. The dispute, which involved thousands of people, had been going on for many years, and it often resulted in violent outbursts. This year had been a particularly dark time, and although there was a ceasefire in place, certain factions of the paramilitary organisations involved were incensed at how the standoff was developing, and there were threats and rumours from both sides. Local residents were adamant that the annual march must not happen and had barricaded Garvaghy Road. Bridie was appalled at some of the things she saw on the news back then, but felt glad that her family was safe.

Despite living where they did, Mick and Bridie never had any involvement in the Troubles. Life was never about creed or colour for the couple. It made no difference to them what religion people were, and they never entertained any thoughts of violence or anger. If they heard something worrying on the news or read a harrowing story in the paper they would simply say a prayer for the families involved and then forget about it. Although it was a very real part of life in County Armagh, it had no real impact on their lives.

As they left the graduation celebration, they all hugged and kissed each other goodbye. Then Michael turned to his parents and said, "I love you both." Mick and Bridie said, in chorus, "I love you right back!" It was the perfect way to finish the night. All fed and watered, safe and sound. But tragically they weren't all safe, and on that fateful night in July 1996 their idyllic lives were about to be torn apart forever.

CHAPTER 14:
No, Lord, No

Bridie and Mick woke up at the caravan on 9th July, looking forward to another hot summer's day. Before making their daily Ulster fry-up and cups of tea, they decided to put Teletext, the rolling news service of the day, on the television. Bridie remembers praying that nobody would have been hurt in relation to the Drumcree standoff.

Mick turned it on and the main headline read, "Taxi man killed in Lurgan." They were shocked, but agreed that if it had been anyone their Michael knew they would have been told. They put the BBC news on just to be sure. The newscaster announced: "The taxi driver murdered in Lurgan, County Armagh, yesterday had just graduated from Queen's University Belfast and was expecting his second child."

At that moment Bridie McGoldrick's world fell apart. This was how she learned that her beloved son Michael had been killed. Her Michael. Murdered. Hearing the worst possible news a parent could ever hear in such a way is unfathomable, yet this was the horrific reality for Bridie and Mick. No words could describe the way they felt as their lives changed instantly and forever. Shortly after they heard this on the news, one of Mick's relatives arrived to confirm their worst nightmare. Their beloved only child had been cruelly taken from them in the early hours of that morning, aged just thirty-one.

Naturally, they were in bits. Absolutely devastated. The caravan park owners had watched the news and came over, but Bridie couldn't even hear what they were saying. She was a complete mess, just inconsolable. She remembers Mick running outside and thumping the ground, screaming up at God that his Son dying on a tree was nothing compared to this, and vowing that he would never smile or laugh again. A doctor appeared from somewhere and tried to get Bridie to take some pills to calm her down, but she knew that if she took one it would make the situation real and her Michael would be dead.

More of Mick's relatives, Paddy and Patricia, arrived to drive them home, but Bridie still couldn't believe what was unfolding. She just kept saying: "It's not our boy. It's not our Michael." She had assumed he would be safe through the Troubles because he was Scottish, and she just couldn't take it in. Shock and horror swept through the caravan park as people there saw the news and made the connection, realising the big affable Michael they all knew and loved was dead.

Martin and his two young brothers were there at the time, and he remembers witnessing their beloved aunt and uncle fall apart. They saw Bridie fall to her knees screaming and people running to the caravan to help. Martin was led away, and eventually all three boys were driven home by a family friend, but he will never forget the overwhelming fear and helplessness they all felt at that moment. It wasn't until they got home that they found out what had happened.

The heartbroken couple arrived home and headed straight over to Michael's house, where a distraught Sadie was doing her best to hold it together for their little girl. The horror for Michael's young wife was unimaginable as she tried to explain to a distraught Emma that her darling daddy was never coming back. Sadie had to find supernatural strength as she carried their unborn baby, actively moving in her womb and just months from being born, while experiencing the greatest heartbreak and shock of her life.

Bridie remembers just sitting there, completely numb. She felt as if she were no longer living in the real world; as though she were watching someone else's life unfold. She could see and hear everything, but none of it seemed real. Somehow her brave daughter-in-law had managed to go to the mortuary to identify and prepare her husband's body. Sadie had also done all she could to make sure Bridie and Mick found out from someone in the family rather than from a police officer.

The house soon began to fill up with relatives, including Jacqueline McGoldrick, who found it a real struggle to see Bridie and Mick so distraught. She saw such pain in their eyes, knowing their one and only child had been taken from them. She just kept thinking how cruel it was; that they had come over to Ireland to be with him and suddenly he was gone. She felt so helpless, as there was really nothing she could say or do to make it any better, and she was also devastated herself to know that Michael was dead.

As they sat in their son's house that evening, Michael's body was brought inside in a coffin; a sight no mother or father should ever have to see. For once in her life, Bridie couldn't think about Sadie or Emma or Mick. She was completely lost, trapped in the darkest place imaginable. Michael looked so peaceful in his coffin, but although she could plainly see him lying there, she was still convinced that her son couldn't be dead. Her head knew the truth but her heart couldn't accept it.

The hours ticked by in an agonising haze as the grief-stricken couple tried to understand what had happened. They simply couldn't begin to fathom it. Shock and horror became their constant companions as the days dragged on, with Bridie existing in a permanent state of disbelief. Even today, many years later, there is a haunted look in her eyes as she shares her story.

The Troubles had reached new and frightening heights that summer, but the McGoldricks were just a normal, working-class Catholic family who bore no one any ill will. They had no links to any paramilitary organisations, and their son had never had any involvement. They simply couldn't understand how this terrible murder had occurred. What had been the point of killing this big, gentle giant who wasn't even Irish?

They eventually found out that Michael hadn't been a specific target. The culprits, from a Loyalist paramilitary group, had simply wanted to kill a Catholic taxi driver, and Michael had just happened to be in the wrong place at the wrong time. Bridie struggled terribly with this. The 'what ifs?' and 'if onlys' drove her crazy as she desperately imagined countless different outcomes and scenarios, but none of them were real. Michael had been murdered and he wasn't coming back.

Michael's colleagues at the taxi firm were all shocked and stunned, particularly as he had been excitedly telling them he was applying for various teaching positions in Lurgan. The big Scotsman was a firm favourite with those he worked alongside. The taxi office workers assumed he had simply headed home to his wife when he didn't check in after his last hire, as the pair were often affectionately described as "lovebirds". Nobody had suspected anything and assumed he was happily at home, having simply forgotten to clock off, but Sadie had raised the alarm when Michael didn't make it back. To everyone's horror, Michael was found early the next morning by a man who was out hunting for rabbits. His body was slumped over the steering wheel and covered in blood.

None of this meant anything to Bridie and Mick at the time, as it was all they could do to take in the horrifying truth that their son was dead; that they would never again hear his laugh or hold him in their arms. It was such a cruel and heartbreaking blow, and at times Bridie didn't think she could go on. Sadly, the horror was completely real and the beleaguered couple had to make their way back to their own little home. They were immediately surrounded by photos of their boy with a world of hope and life in his eyes.

There was a steady stream of visitors, family members and friends who came to show their love and to support the couple through their grief. But despite having a houseful of people who were incredibly generous and absolutely heartbroken for them, Bridie was barely aware of what was happening around her. People brought so much food over they had trays of it piled high in the kitchen, but neither Mick nor Bridie felt like eating. They were still in shock, still numb from the horror of it, and despite having full-blown conversations with people Bridie wasn't able to take anything in.

Again, a doctor came to the house and suggested Bridie take some pills to help get her through, but again she refused, preferring to cling to some irrational hope that it was all a nightmare she would wake from at some point.

Mick was also completely devastated, as the bond he had enjoyed with his only child had been just as strong and precious. He felt as though he would never get over it, and he just couldn't get his head around the fact that someone, anyone, had chosen to kill Michael. Memories flooded over him at all hours as he tried to be strong for Bridie, Sadie and his darling Emma, but he just couldn't conceal his anger at God, who he felt had let them down badly. He and Michael were very similar and had the same sense of humour, which crept into every conversation. They loved to laugh, wind Bridie up, play football, watch their beloved Celtic and just hang out together. They weren't just father and son, they were friends too, and Michael's murder ripped Mick's heart apart.

When Christina received the phone call telling her the horrendous news it was simply too terrible to take in and seemed completely unreal. It was so shocking to see the national news reports with Michael's car covered in police tape and images of her cousin's smiling face on the screen. Christina's heart broke for her aunt and uncle, and she was filled with a sense of grief and mourning that rocked her to her core. The hardest part was not being able to do anything about it; not being able to bring him back.

Michael had been more like a brother than a cousin while they were growing up in Glasgow. Her mind instantly relived their idyllic childhood, the pranks they had played on each other, the running games, the chases, the dares, the conversations, and the hopes and dreams as they got older. She just couldn't believe Michael's life had been snuffed out so quickly and so mercilessly. She couldn't accept that he had been so cruelly taken from them. It was the kind of thing she was used to reading about other people in the newspapers or watching on the TV, only this time it was her big, clumsy cousin. The heartbreak she felt spread through the whole family.

The business of arranging Michael's funeral was handled by Sadie and Mick. The young widow was so strong and determined in the face of such devastating loss, and Mick provided as much support as possible. Everyone in their local community, and in fact the whole country, had heard about the senseless killing of this loveable family man, and people from all walks of life started sending cards, flowers and messages.

Mick was down at the police station attending to some legalities when one of the police officers passed on his condolences. He commented that it was the worst possible news any father could hear. Mick thought for a minute, then replied: "No, the worst possible news would be hearing that my boy had shot and murdered someone else's son." Even at this time of intense pain, his sense of integrity shone through. Mick was devastated, yet he still understood that if Michael had inflicted this horror on another family it would have been beyond comprehension.

The reality of their loss was overwhelming, and on the Saturday before Michael's funeral the pair had reached their limit. They asked all their friends and relatives to give them some space, explaining they needed time to themselves. In the wee small hours, alone in their bedroom when they could talk to each other candidly, Bridie and Mick decided they couldn't go on; that they didn't want to live without Michael. The ache in their hearts was too painful, and it felt as though they were drowning in an abyss of pain and sorrow. The grief was constant, like a black cloud that wouldn't go away. They weren't thinking about Sadie, little Emma or the unborn child; they could only think about Michael. The couple desperately wanted to see and be with him, and at that point, the lowest of their lives, they wanted to die. So that afternoon, side by side in the living room, holding hands, they got themselves ready to commit suicide.

They set all of Bridie's arthritis, stomach and pain medications out on the table and planned to take enough to end their lives. It was the only course of action they could think of. Thankfully, it didn't go according to plan! Mick had gone to make himself a sandwich because he was scared he might vomit the pills back up if his stomach were empty, which would scupper their suicide bid. The house was full of every kind of sandwich filling, bread, cake and biscuit imaginable, yet they had no butter, so Mick made a thick sandwich on dry bread. They said their loving goodbyes to one another and prepared to end it all after Mick had eaten his sandwich.

However, as the bread was so dry he couldn't swallow it very easily. Bridie heard Mick start choking as he began to eat it, and they both panicked. She started to pat his back vigorously as he motioned for her to help him. His face was full of terror as he struggled to breathe, and Bridie was thumping him violently, desperately trying to dislodge the piece of bread that was stuck. It was a scary experience and Bridie didn't want him to die. She knew she had to do whatever it took to stop him choking to death, and Mick was also desperate not to go. Eventually, the offending piece of dough was removed.

This was an unexpected turn of events, and their joint reaction brought the couple to their senses. All of their instincts were telling them to preserve their lives rather than end them. It sobered them up, and Mick began to laugh loudly. They were both aware that it had been the least successful suicide attempt ever, and they were glad of it. Then Mick grasped Bridie's hand tightly and began to cry out to God. They were distraught, and it was clear that they couldn't cope with the grief alone. They both fell to their knees in front of the cross in their house and begged God to help them. Mick admitted they were a couple of fools, then prayed and asked God to forgive them. They stayed like that, crying out and pleading with God, for a long time. They both knew that he had heard and would answer them. Then Mick took her hand and helped her upstairs, where they lay on the bed exhausted and fell into a deep, peaceful sleep for the first time.

A strength of sorts came to the beleaguered pair, but the reality of the ensuing funeral preparations continued to be a necessary heartache for Bridie. She and Mick realised people just wanted the couple to know they were there for them, but they still couldn't take it all in. Margaret and John came over from Scotland together, and aside from the Saturday of the suicide attempt Margaret never left Bridie's side. People kept telling stories about Michael; of how he had impacted their lives and how much they loved him. While this was well-intentioned, it felt weird for Bridie. He was her boy, and she didn't want anyone else talking about him. Everyone was being so kind and sympathetic, but she didn't want their sympathy; she wanted her boy! Bridie still couldn't accept that she would never see him again.

Often it was the silly things that came to her mind at that time of intense grief. On the eve of his funeral, she found herself thinking: 'Oh son, your hair will never grow back now!'

The years have never diminished the ache in her heart left by Michael's passing, and she still yearns to see, hold and speak to him again. The weight of grief continues to hang heavily around this loving mother's broken heart.

The Troubles continued to rage around them, and the Drumcree standoff was garnering worldwide publicity. Bridie, Mick and Sadie were hounded by the press, with reporters hungry for column inches from the grieving family. Michael's murder shocked and horrified everyone with any sense of compassion, but for those who were entrenched in the fight for their perceived cause it was seen as an act of terrorism that had made a significant impact. The world waited for the next move. How would this forlorn family avenge their son?

Against all the odds, Mick also felt a strange joy on the morning of his son's funeral. It was a deep, beautiful, uncontrollable joy that filled his soul and couldn't have been manufactured. He was absolutely certain that God was giving him a foretaste of the perfection of heaven. But while Mick was incredibly strong, Bridie was in pieces. Her body was going through the motions, but her brain was numb. She couldn't understand how Michael could look so handsome and peaceful in his coffin when he was gone forever. She still didn't know the full extent of his injuries at this time, as Sadie hadn't wanted her to be tormented any further. All she knew was that he had been fatally shot. It was so cruel and senseless, she just couldn't get her head around it.

The family had to say their last goodbyes to Michael's body before they left for the chapel, and it felt as though what was left of Bridie's heart was being ripped to pieces. All she could do was stand there, with tears streaming down her face, repeating internally: 'I love you, son. I love you.' Mick put his hand over Michael's hand and simply said: "Bye, son. See you in heaven." Then he brought the coffin lid down. He went downstairs to find a piece of paper to write something down, tucking it away in his pocket.

Given the furore surrounding Michael's killing, the media interest was intense. The funeral was covered on all the major news channels in Northern Ireland, the rest of the UK and even in the US. The chapel was packed with friends, family members and many who had heard about and been moved by the senseless killing. The air was fragrant with the smell of flowers as the chapel and undertakers had been swamped with bouquets of condolences. There were lovely readings and hymns, but the whole funeral went by in a haze for Bridie. She was unable to take it all in and wasn't aware of who was there or what was happening.

Too upset to go to the graveside, Bridie waited in the funeral car, unable to watch as her boy was finally laid to rest. She couldn't bear to see them put Michael in the ground; it was too agonising. She sat in the car, thinking about her son and wishing she could have him in her home once again. She knew that he would have put his arms around her as she stood at the sink and say: "How's my wee Bridie? Sure, I'm a nice guy, amn't I, Mum?" just as he had when he was a boy and wanted a cuddle. Her arms ached to hold him again.

The driver was a nice young guy, and he leaned over to ask if she wanted a smoke, which she did. He told Bridie his heart was breaking for her and that she reminded him of his mammy. As she sat there, unable to watch her son being interred, Mick was preparing to address the gathered media. Still chasing the family for their reaction to the murder and for pictures of them saying their goodbyes, a crowd of journalists and photographers had gathered at the chapel and by the graveside. Television crews from around the world were begging for a comment, such was the powder keg the Drumcree standoff had become. Everyone wanted to know how this previously unknown couple would react to the brutal killing of their son.

Mick walked over to the microphones and took out the little piece of paper he had written on while he was saying goodbye to Michael at the house. It simply said: "Forgive them."

Looking right into the cameras, he addressed both sides of the sectarian divide and said: "As I bury my son, both of you bury your pride. I don't want any mother or father going through what my wife and I have went through today. I've watched my daughter-in-law, I've watched my grandchild go through hell. Don't do it. Please stop this.

Bury your pride with my boy. To those who've done this, I and my family forgive you."

CHAPTER 15:
Forgiven Much

The shock of this statement registered worldwide. How could a grieving father, the head of a family torn apart by cruelty, stand up at his son's funeral and forgive the people who had killed him? There was an air of disbelief, and all the news reports that night focused on this humble man from Country Armagh who had offered forgiveness at the most horrific time in his life, and to the very people who had robbed him of his much-loved only child.

As Mick was saying goodbye to Michael in the coffin, he had been reminded of God losing his own Son, Jesus. He also remembered that God was quick to give his grace and forgiveness to those who needed it and realised he couldn't withhold these things from others. He was speaking for both of them when he said those words, though Bridie still has to go to God daily to receive this incredible forgiveness for the men who had killed her Michael. She also recognised that this forgiveness wasn't hers to give; it had to come from God.

Mick had gone from being angry with God to operating on an inner strength nobody had known he possessed. The day after the funeral he cried out to God for help as he walked the dog, desperately needing a touch from the Lord. In that moment he was filled with uncontrollable joy and couldn't stop laughing. He returned to the house to find two priests who had come to offer support, and, bright as a button, Mick declared that he was holier than the pope, and that if he died there and then he knew he would go straight to heaven. The boldness of the statement may have been uncharacteristic, but it was definitely sincere.

Immediately afterwards he went outside and a dark, horrible presence overcame him, taking him into the pit of darkness and despair. He had been afraid and suddenly felt cold, and he knew he was experiencing something of hell. It felt incredibly real and absolutely vile. Mick felt so alone and helpless, and he realised that God was the only one who could lift him out. He began to pray some of the Acts of Contrition; prayers he had said hundreds of times before as a Catholic, though he had never meant them the way he did that day. It was as if Mick needed to confess every wrong thing he had ever done and receive God's forgiveness. He knew in his heart that God was able to save him, and in that moment he also knew he would. Mick was brought up out of that place by the greatest sense of love and warmth he had ever felt, and he knew that it was God.

Bridie witnessed this, as Mick had fallen to his hands and knees. Although she wanted to help him, she instinctively knew that this was part of Mick's journey, and that it was between him and God. While they shared everything as a married couple, every person's walk with the Lord is personal, and this was clearly part of Mick's.

Bridie knew that only God was capable of giving that ability to forgive. They had been asking God to help and hold them. It wasn't humanly possible to forgive those who had murdered their son, yet by the grace of God they were somehow able to do it. They knew it was a gift they had been given, and they were prepared to speak it out. As soon as they decided to release this grace a healing seemed to come to the couple. It wasn't a magical thing that instantly made everything OK, and they weren't given a release from the pain, which was and still is awful, but God seemed to give them a way to cope by offering grace where it had previously seemed impossible.

For the rest of the family, and for those watching the story unfold on the various news channels, Mick and Bridie's reaction was incomprehensible. Jacqueline had been a close family member for years, but she felt as if she was watching something absolutely amazing unfold. She simply couldn't understand how they had been able to forgive Michael's killers. It was hard for her to see it, yet she was truly inspired by them.

Having grown up in Glasgow, Jacqueline had experienced division there, but nothing on this scale. She had never been able to understand why someone would be killed because of a dispute over religion. She was heavily pregnant at this time, and, like Sadie, was due in October. This only served to make her heart ache more for Michael's widow and grieving parents.

Despite the depth of tragedy they were facing, the door to the McGoldrick house remained open, as it always had been. However, all those who were close to the couple and Sadie were at a loss as to how they could help. What words could be found to ease a mother's broken heart or a widow's pain?

Another person whose world had been completely rocked was Emma. At just seven years old she had been especially close to her dad and couldn't really take in what was happening. She was often very quiet, clearly trying to process what she was experiencing. Sadie was there for her every step of the way, holding her close despite her own heartbreak. She had to carry on each day for Emma's sake and for her unborn child; the baby she and Michael had so longed for and been delighted to conceive. Bridie's heart went out to her young daughter-in-law at this terrible time.

The whole community of Craigavon was aware of the amazing couple's stance. Some in their family circle couldn't understand it, but Bridie was convinced that God was asking them to extend to others the forgiveness he had freely given to them. It was a supernatural grace that allowed her to do so in the face of crippling grief and disbelief. This grief completely envelops Bridie at times, and she still feels an agony and darkness that pulls her in. But she is now aware when it happens and asks God to help her get out, as the loss of her only son has left a gaping wound in her heart that no earthly thing can fill.

On the 12th of July, the day after the funeral, Mick announced to Bridie that they were going back to the caravan. Bridie was reluctant, thinking it a crazy idea, but Mick insisted. He sensed they needed to reclaim their special place of beauty and peace before it became too difficult to return, forever linked to Michael's murder. Family and friends gathered to say goodbye and, with Margaret and John heading back to Scotland, Bridie and Mick set off.

The fact that it was the 12th of July – the pinnacle of the Orange Order's marching season – meant the streets across Belfast were teeming with people and traffic was a nightmare. Cars were checked for bombs, ammunition and even people. Folks were searched if the police considered them in any way suspicious, and there was a terrible atmosphere of hatred and fear.

As they were heading away from Belfast, the streets around them began to look deserted. In fact, the only people they met were the police officers who stopped them. Bridie guessed that the officers recognised Mick because they kindly told the couple about a little-known shortcut they had never heard of, and the pair miraculously made their way to the caravan without any problems. It was meant to be.

When they got to Warrenpoint the pair went inside and closed the door, needing to be on their own. A rush of pain and emotion swept over them as they shut out the world and spent a few precious hours together in the special place they both adored. Memories of that awful morning when they received the earth-shattering news still flit across Bridie's face as she talks about it today, as the tentacles of the evil act reach down through the years, yet the steely determination that runs through her like a girder is also evident, and the couple's desire to be there for Sadie, Emma and the unborn baby drove them on.

The following day, Mick insisted they join friends for a meal at the nearby pub they often visited when they were in Warrenpoint. Neither had eaten much since the fateful day they had heard the news, and although Bridie couldn't face the thought of it, Mick was adamant and refused to allow Bridie to sit in the caravan alone as she had requested. While Bridie barely managed to get through a cup of tea, she fondly remembers watching her husband scoff down a whole meal. Mick ate everything on the plate, then said: "Thank you, Lord."

Meanwhile, the press had found out about the caravan and descended on Warrenpoint in pursuit of the couple. Mick and Bridie prayed they would go away and leave them alone... and they did! Miraculously, the reporters left without a single photo or interview.

Mick had decided that he wanted to start reading the Bible, so off he went to nearby Rostrevor and bought one. He became completely engrossed by it, reading for hours and hours and taking in every word. There was a Christian centre nearby that was open to Catholics and Protestants who wanted to pray for peace and unity in Ireland, particularly during the marching season. Mick kept saying that he just had to go inside, as he needed to talk to someone. Ever loyal, Bridie agreed to go with him in the hope of satisfying this longing.

When they went inside, a prayer meeting specifically about the Troubles and the marches was taking place. Those inside were very welcoming to the couple, although they had no idea who Mick and Bridie were at that point.

Mick spoke to the leader of the Christian centre, Cecil Kerr, a man who was very happy to make time for the couple. Bridie was happy to see her husband so enthusiastic about his faith but wasn't able to share his excitement. Mick spoke to Cecil and told him everything that had happened. He explained that God was doing something inside him and that he had to know what it was. Mick described the horrible experience he had endured back home, and how afraid and desperate he had felt, and Cecil asked whether it had felt like a snake shedding its skin. Mick said that was exactly how it had felt, sensing that God had led him to this particular meeting on this particular night.

Cecil was a patient and humble man of God. He told Mick it was the Holy Spirit at work and asked if he wanted to invite the Spirit into his life. Mick was totally ready for it, so he asked Cecil and a few others who were there to pray with him and to ask God to come more fully into his life. They prayed for the Holy Spirit to come, and Mick was changed forever that night.

Aware that they were all praying for her to find peace and strength, Bridie was less keen. She was grateful for their compassion, but she didn't want their prayers. She just wanted her boy back! She was sitting there feeling a little detached when a kind-looking man sat beside her and asked if he could lay hands on her. She agreed, still feeling somewhat remote from it all. All of a sudden she felt a wonderful sense of peace flood through her. It was unreal. She knew that something or someone was there, touching her soul deeply and in a strangely beautiful way. She instinctively said: "Is that you, God?"

Knowing this wasn't something she was capable of stirring up herself, Bridie was suddenly mesmerised. The man, who turned out to be a priest, still had his hands on her, and she began to feel a burning sensation on her shoulders. It was such a lovely warm feeling. Later on, the same man said to her: "Wow! When I was praying for you it felt like you were on fire. The heat coming from you was intense." Bridie knew it was God. She knew he had touched her, and she knew that, just like Mick, she would never be the same again.

The McGoldricks were experiencing such deep and conflicting emotions at this time. They felt heartbroken, distraught and lost in a sea of grief, yet at the same time a new and very real sense of hope was growing in their hearts. They both felt the grace of God flooding through them. As lifelong Catholics who regularly went to Mass, they had always believed in God but had held a very distant view of him; an image of the imposing Almighty who was watching and waiting for any sinful behaviour that would exclude them from heaven. They had sought to please the Lord from an ingrained sense of fear and duty. Yet right at the worst, most horrific time in their lives, they started to experience a deep love and affection they couldn't comprehend, and it was happening to them both in equally great yet distinct ways.

Something had touched Bridie that night in the Christian fellowship that she had never experienced before. At the point of her greatest loss and most desperate need, she knew that God loved her in ways she had never really understood before. She couldn't verbalise the way she was feeling, but right after burying Michael, when all she could do was try to get through each day, she was being comforted. She knew that only God could bring that sort of peace.

Meanwhile, Mick's desire to read the Bible had become insatiable, and spent hours poring over each chapter and verse. He wanted to know more about this God who had reached down to him in his darkest moment; this God who was bringing him hope and even joy, when not long beforehand he had contemplated suicide. Hour after hour Mick would read the Bible, pray, read some more and memorise verses. He was so excited by the truth he was reading in this amazing book.

Another book that had a massive influence in Mick's life was Prison to Praise by Merlin Carothers, which speaks of praising God regardless of circumstances. This was something Mick and Bridie both understood and held on to.

Cecil Kerr became a great encouragement to the couple. He was always ready to answer Mick's questions and pray with them both. He soon began to give Bridie the kind of support she had been craving, playing a pivotal role in her emotional and spiritual journey. She immediately sensed he was a very gentle person who really cared about them, and it was easier to open up to him because he wasn't part of the family and had never known Michael.

Not everyone understood the couple's decision to forgive. Many people wondered how it was possible for them to know that their only son had been cruelly murdered and not feel any loathing or hatred. Once again, the answer was in their new-found faith; in the love of God they had experienced in their own lives. Bridie has no doubt it was the grace of God alone that gave them the strength to do so. While Bridie and Mick were devastated and horrified by their loss, their new closeness to God enabled them to hold on to him and do the seemingly impossible. They didn't forgive the killers for the killers' sakes, but because they knew the God they loved so dearly had given up his own Son for them. They knew they had received grace and mercy for their wrongdoings, and that God was teaching them through the Bible to offer the same love and forgiveness he had offered them. It wasn't easy for Bridie to forgive Michael's murderers all those years ago, and it's no less difficult today. Only by the grace of God has it been possible.

CHAPTER 16:
From Death To Life

A new chapter had begun for Mick and Bridie. Life without their precious only child would never be the same, and they were both heartbroken, but they also knew they had to go on, even it was just for Sadie, Emma and the new baby's sake. Bridie describes Sadie as a "wee trouper", who was also pushing on through her pain. Sadie was fully committed to bringing Emma and Andrew up well, and her in-laws were delighted to help in whatever way they could. She confided to Bridie years later that while she was organising Michael's funeral she had bought a family plot, saying the McGoldricks had been inseparable in life and that she didn't want to separate them in death. This meant Mick and Bridie could be buried with their boy when their time came.

Bridie was so touched by this thoughtful gesture, but it also made her realise what Sadie had lost. All of the couple's plans and dreams were gone. She had nothing but admiration for the way Sadie coped at this time, and so appreciated her grieving daughter-in-law's kindness to them. Emma was coping in her own little way. She missed her daddy terribly, as she had been his princess, but she was extremely brave. Mick and Bridie knew Michael would have wanted them to be there for his little family and to love them just the way they would have if he hadn't been killed. They wanted to have their arms wide open to pour love and hope into their shattered brood, and that's exactly what they did.

Andrew Michael McGoldrick was born on 3rd October weighing 8lbs, the exact same weight as his father, who had died just three months earlier. This was a time of great happiness and celebration, but it was very much tempered by the events of that awful day in July. Bridie was so glad Andrew had arrived safely and delighted that Michael had a son, yet it was so sad at the same time. Looking down at the healthy little bundle of joy, she hated the fact that his daddy wasn't there to enjoy these happy moments.

Andrew was a lovely baby, and he looked just like Michael had as a newborn. It was a tough time for everyone, and emotions were running high. Sadie was extremely strong once again, but Bridie knew her heart was breaking because her husband wasn't there to see their gorgeous son. It was a sad start for a new baby, yet Andrew never wanted for anything, either in terms of love or material things. He was the apple of his mum's eye .Andrew McGoldrick was a godsend for the whole family, bringing joy during a very dark time.

This little boy would never know his father, but he was surrounded by enough love and kindness to know that he was wanted, and Andrew was told plenty of tales about his father's short life. Evil couldn't rob this family of its history, and just as Michael McGoldrick had been born, raised and lived in nothing but love and encouragement, so were Emma and Andrew. Mick and Bridie were determined to ensure that Michael's little family was nurtured in the same way.

Their roles as grandparents changed after Michael's death, but they got to see Sadie and the children all the time. They encouraged Sadie to go back to work, as it was too painful for her to be in the house day in, day out. Bridie and Mick watched Andrew while she was at work from Monday until Wednesday while Sadie's mum Pauline looked after Emma. It was a difficult period of adjustment for the whole family, but somehow they got through it. The horrific tragedy had left its mark on them all, and for at least a month after Andrew was born Bridie would sit up all night when he was staying with them and watch him sleep, scared that something terrible might happen to him. This response may be typical for some grandmothers, but for one who had just buried her own son, looking after this precious little boy felt like an even greater responsibility.

As ever when life was tough, Bridie was Mick's rock, but she also leaned on him to get through these difficult weeks and months. Although he was also grieving, he had been completely changed by his encounter with God, and he had a strength about him that gave Bridie a real reassurance when she was struggling the most.

Drawing on his growing faith, Mick was a different man and Bridie was delighted to watch him go from strength to strength in his walk with God. It was especially nice for Bridie, as she had been encouraging Mick in this area for years, teaching him all she had learned during her years of faithful service. Bridie could see that her husband finally understood the faith she had always held.

In one moment of enthusiasm, clearly delighted with and confident in his deepening relationship with God, he declared: "Get in behind me, Bridie, because I'm going straight to heaven."

Quick as a flash, she replied: "I know you are, love. I'm pushing you!" This served as a gentle reminder that his wise wee wummin had been right about God all along!

For friends and family it was like a journey into the unknown at this time, and they wondered how on earth their beloved Mick and Bridie could go on. Christina knew their strength could only have come from one source, and she could see that their faith was absolutely solid. But while she was also a Christian, she constantly found herself asking how a loving God could have taken Michael from them.

As she watched her Aunty Bunty coping with everything life threw at her, she could see how real and strong her relationship with God was. Bridie was hurting so deeply, yet she pressed into her faith, drawing admiration from her family members and friends, who could do nothing more than be there when they were needed. Christina was so proud of her aunty, who refused to let heartache and violence rob her of her beliefs or compassion.

Meanwhile, Jacqueline was experiencing major changes in her own life. She suffered terribly with back pain and deteriorating health, and was never able to return to work after her fourth son was born. She spent as much time as possible with Bridie and Mick, and even though they were in unimaginable pain they always made Jacqueline and her family feel welcome. Her boys loved being there, and they always came home full of giggles and great stories.

One source of giggles came when Bridie was asked to do a simple favour for Jacqueline, which involved taking a urine sample to the pharmacist to see if Jacqueline was pregnant again. The clearly middle-aged Bridie couldn't resist the opportunity to make other people smile, so she dramatically begged the assistant as she handed it over to make sure it was negative, as she couldn't face being pregnant at her age. She said she would return the next day for the 'bad' news.

As she entered the shop the next day, the same assistant ran out the back to bring out a chair, which she motioned for Bridie to sit on. Then the pharmacist walked round to tell her it was positive. There were smiles of relief all round when she confessed to having brought the sample in for Jacqueline.

Mick and Bridie had to rebuild their lives day by day. Their spiritual life had been hugely impacted, and they were both being changed and renewed. However, while they were moving in the same direction by the same God, they were experiencing him in very different ways. Mick admitted he had only really gone to chapel regularly beforehand to please Bridie rather than out of any genuine desire or faith on his part. Meanwhile, her attendance had been based on a fear of going to hell, not a real love for God.

Bridie had her own epiphany in the lead-up to Christmas. Although part of her was dreading the festive season, she busied herself putting up Christmas decorations, including a nativity set. Baby Jesus always stayed in the drawer until midnight on Christmas Eve; a tradition she had stuck to over the years. As she was adding him to the scene this particular year, the words the priest had spoken at Mass the previous Sunday came back to her mind. He had been talking about Jesus being born as a real baby, fragile and vulnerable; a baby who would have needed to be picked up and held, just like every other baby. As Bridie held the baby Jesus figurine in her hand, something just clicked. She felt a warmth and love flood through her from head to toe, and she understood that, rather than just sitting there in judgement and wrath, God looked at her as his child and he wanted to love and protect her. She knew in that instant that he was truly her Father in heaven, embodying all the love and kindness towards his children that she had felt for her Michael. She felt love like she never had before, and the fear of God, which had scared her at times, left. She no longer feared a cruel or disappointed heavenly Father; she knew she was his beloved Bridie and that God was never going to let her go. Bridie had previously tried to earn God's love, but she discovered that it was freely given and never-ending.

This realisation was pivotal in shaping her into the woman she is today. Whatever she has gone through, and there has been a great deal of struggle, Bridie has faced life with a deep assurance that God loves and is looking out for her. Although many things in life have momentarily shaken her, nothing has been able to uproot Bridie's understanding of who she is in God's eyes. It was so special for Bridie to be able to share this new understanding of God with Mick. She felt really blessed, and they started going to chapel every day and really looking forward to it. They loved being around people who felt the same way about their faith. With baby Andrew in tow while Emma was at school, the couple became well-known faces in the parish. The congregation was all too well aware of the tragedy the family was bravely coming to terms with, as well as the depth and passion of God for this pair of faithful worshippers.

The whole country now knew their names, and the press was still relentlessly pursuing them. They were also invited to speak in various churches, on the radio and on television. At first Mick did all the speaking, while Bridie preferred to take a supportive back seat. Mick always knew how to share their story with grace and love, whoever the audience happened to be. He spoke with such compassion and common sense that he made an impact wherever he went. However, God had also given wee Bunty from the Gorbals a voice, and her position on the sidelines was finally relinquished when she agreed to join Mick on the platform one night. She didn't really have a plan; she just spoke from the heart, from a mother's point of view. She told them the murder had broken her heart, and that she just kept asking "Why me? Why my boy?" She was honest about the heartache and pain, and even the fact that she hadn't wanted to carry on living. She didn't try to hide her failings or weaknesses, but instead simply shared her story in all its messiness.

The impact her words had on those listening that first night was enormous. So many people responded to it, and crowds of people came to talk with her afterwards, some of whom had also lost children. She was astounded that she had been able to reach them, despite feeling as though she was nobody special. Those listening had found her honesty, bravery and conviction about the saving grace of Jesus inspiring and infectious. It warmed Bridie's heart that she could help others simply by telling her story. Bridie is unstoppable once she gets going, delighting in telling everyone about her precious boy. Her story never fails to inspire, especially consider the magnitude of the task she faced in forgiving those responsible. Bridie's soft, tender heart understood love and loss, and she connected well with people, especially other women. She is often able to stop people in their tracks with just a sentence or two, usually something along the lines of: "Ach, away with you. Sure, God knows best and He won't let you down."

They received several requests to appear on TV and radio shows, which they mainly turned down, but on one occasion they felt compelled to go on TV. Bridie spoke boldly on a show where people were arguing back and forth about the Troubles and whether or not they should be fighting or bearing arms. She simply said: "I think we should take up arms. Then she held out her arms. "These arms. We should take them to each other and then we will see what happens."

The debate completely changed she encouraged those listening to move beyond their anger and try to love and respect one another; maybe even to hug and offer comfort instead of hating and tearing each other down. Bridie knew the words she spoke were not her own, but from God himself.

The question of forgiveness had been quickly addressed as far as Mick and Bridie were concerned, but there still a sense of mystery in relation to whom were they forgiving and why these people had taken Michael's life. At first there were no strong suspects.

Although the murder was clearly linked to the Drumcree standoff, no names had been put forward. Frustratingly for the couple, and for all who had known and loved Michael, it would be five years before anyone was brought to justice.

Bridie and Mick chose not to dwell on the murder. Instead, they grabbed the opportunity to help raise Andrew and Emma – their beautiful grandchildren and Michael's most precious legacy – with both hands. Although it was heartbreaking to think that Andrew would never meet his doting father here on earth, and Emma would have to live the rest of her earthly life without her dad, they concentrated on being the best grandparents they could be. Life was busy, and words such as revenge and recompense simply didn't form part of their vocabulary. Sadie remained close and continued to work hard to provide for her little family, ever grateful for the help and care Bridie and Mick showed her. She didn't allow her own heartache to make her bitter; quite the opposite, in fact. Sadie became a counsellor to help other families get through difficult times. She also volunteered with the Samaritans, offering a lifeline at the end of the phone for folks who were struggling. Jacqueline went on to have her fifth child and only girl, Caoimhe, who proved to be another great Blessing in the McGoldricks' lives.

This new season of life also brought with it new friendships for Mick and Bridie, and one man who entered their lives at this time was about to take them on a journey that would change their lives forever.

CHAPTER 17:
East Meets Best

Mick met a man named Tom Lennon one night at a prayer meeting in Lurgan. Tom was heading up a charity called United Christian Aid, which helped the poor in Eastern Europe, and it turned out to be a fateful, fruitful meeting. Mick was impressed by what the charity was doing and told Tom he would love to do something similar. In fact, he was so enthusiastic about helping the poor that Tom invited Mick on board right away.

When he returned home, Mick said to Bridie: "Our Michael's safe in heaven and doesn't need us any more, but God is showing me there are other children who do need help, and I want to help some of them." Bridie was really touched by this and wholeheartedly agreed that she wanted to do the same. They had both heard about a deep need in Romania and wanted to help in any way they could. They decided to gather clothes and goods that would be helpful for those living there, asking in the Belfast, Craigavon, Lurgan and Portadown communities if anyone wanted to donate. Their house was soon overflowing with donations as neighbours, friends, family members and complete strangers started bringing bags filled with all sorts of items for them to send to the poor and needy.

The couple quickly realised this venture had much greater potential than they had first thought. The logical next step was to find a storage facility, as they were receiving such a large volume of goods, so they began to pray for suitable premises. It wasn't long before a woman got in touch, out of the blue, and offered them the use of a derelict building, which became their storehouse. Bridie was excited, impressed and even a little overwhelmed by people's willingness to give, especially as it wasn't always the wealthiest who gave most generously.

One of the reasons Mick and Tom had clicked straight away was the faith the pair shared and lived by. That first unexpected meeting spawned a lifelong friendship, which was underpinned by the great respect they had for one another. Led by the Holy Spirit, the two men knew God had asked them to do this work. In a vision Mick had, God told him to love all the children he brought across his path. Mick had loved his own child deeply, and God gave him a huge heart for every child he met through the charity. Nothing was too much trouble for him, and he worked tirelessly, giving everything he had to the cause.

The charity served to unite Protestants and Catholics in Northern Ireland as they joined forces to help those living in abject poverty. Some goods were gathered in Orange halls, others in parochial chapel halls, but eventually all the volunteers came together as one to give to those in need. It seemed completely fitting that the McGoldricks should become involved in such an organisation, and such was Mick's enthusiasm and drive that he soon became one of the charity's directors. It wasn't long before, under Mick's enthusiastic directorship, United Christian Aid introduced a family sponsorship scheme for the poor and broken in Romania. The folks around them paid a monthly sum that went directly to a family in need, and United Christian Aid provided newsletters and regular updates about the sponsored families in return.

Mick was a disciplined man, his days in the army having drilled him well. Every morning he would walk Snowy, eat his breakfast, then sit down to do all the necessary paperwork. Mick saw real beauty in sponsoring families, and his dedication to that segment of the charity was unshakeable. While Mick was a gentle, laidback man in most areas of life, slow to speak and quick to listen, he was completely driven and tenacious when it came to helping the needy. He was also very effective as part of a team. The love and affection he had for his wife and 'teammate', Bridie, had stood him in good stead for this work, and it was important to Mick that she was on board with him, providing wonderful support as always.

In typical style, Bridie also threw herself into this new venture and was equally happy to help those in need. The pair committed their time and efforts to spreading the word about the plight of the many people forgotten by communism in Eastern Europe, encouraging members of the local community to get on board. It was such a wonderful time of guidance from God for the pair. They were still faithfully gathering clothes, banking money and reaching out to people in Northern Ireland, but the Lord was starting to make it increasingly clear that he had plans for them over in Romania as well.

Bridie lovingly waved Mick off on his and Tom's first trip over. She was a little less joyful on his return, however, as Mick arrived home terribly thin after barely eating. It turned out he had given away most of the food he had to those around them. He had barely slept on that first trip either, so he returned home looking very drawn and tired. He was desperate to hug her, having missed her terribly, but Bridie couldn't believe the state of him and told him to get washed first as the smell was enough to knock someone out!

She wasn't the only one who noticed his altered appearance. Bridie was shocked when, just before the next trip, a man came to the front door and gave Mick £100. He made it clear that it wasn't for the charity; it was for Mick to buy food. The couple tried to say no but the man wouldn't hear of it, so they reluctantly accepted the money. No sooner had they shut the front door than a knock came at the back door, and they found a man waiting there with another £100 for the same reason. They were both deeply touched by the genuine concern for Mick among the local community, and more than a little embarrassed.

One time during the first trip, the driver of the big van they were travelling in had selfishly taken up the spare bunk with his luggage and wouldn't allow Mick to lie down. As it wasn't his van and he didn't speak the language, there was nothing Mick could do but wait. As he sat there, listening to the man's snores and sweltering in the heat, he opened a window to allow some air in, unwittingly allowing a load of mosquitoes inside. The next day the driver was covered in bites from head to toe, which amused Mick no end. "God really loves me," he stated, "I haven't a single bite." The next day, however, he emerged from the lorry covered from head to toe in bites himself. When he got home, Mick declared to Bridie as she smothered on the calamine that God had wanted to teach him that he loved the van driver just as much as him!

It wasn't long before Mick and Tom were travelling out to Eastern Europe six times a year to distribute the goods they had gathered from across Northern Ireland. Each time they hired an interpreter to make sure they were aware of people's needs and to ensure that things ran smoothly. The journey was long and arduous by van, but the two men were delighted to be helping folks who had nothing. Mick's eyes had been opened to the horrors of poverty there, particularly during the first trip, but he was also filled with joy that they were doing something to make a difference.

Despite her own physical pain and limitations, Bridie was determined to travel to Romania as well. Although she didn't make it out on every trip, she went often enough for her heart to be forever melted on behalf of the poor in this part of the world. The sights she saw absolutely horrified her. Whole families would be huddled together in filthy, makeshift shelters, and she saw people literally living in the mud. Nothing could have prepared her for the desperation, and her heart broke for the people she met. It shocked her to see the emptiness in their blank eyes, which appeared so cold and lifeless. There were so many tales of horror, but Bridie could never forget seeing one five-year-old boy wearing nothing but an old baggy jumper with no underwear or shoes. It was freezing cold and the child had no protection from the elements.

Bridie quickly learned not to make snap judgements about people early on, particularly when she was greeted by a number of tables laden with food in one of the villages. She began to wonder whether there was really a great need there, but she didn't discover until later that these people had brought out everything they owned as a way of saying thanks. They had nothing left for themselves, yet they wanted these kind strangers with their funny accents to know they were appreciated.

Given their own heartache and loss, the McGoldricks could have been forgiven for pulling back and letting others go to the coal face, yet the needs they saw were so great and touching they found a strength and purpose to carry on. On one occasion, however, Bridie's deepening relationship with the Lord was severely tested, and once again she experienced deep heartache. She had made it her mission to visit as many people as possible on the trip, especially those who were sick. She was visiting a boy of about eleven who had AIDS, and he was so ill that Bridie just picked him up and nursed him lovingly in her arms. His little body was so weak he just lay there, unmoving, until eventually he died right there in her arms.

Anyone holding a child in their arms as they took their final breath would have found it truly terrible, but coming so soon after her son's tragic death this incident could have sent Bridie into a place of overwhelming grief or rage… and it almost did. She knew a prayer meeting had been set up for that night but refused to go. Instead, she sat there on her own, asking God how he could have let that happen. What had the little boy ever done to him? Why had he allowed her to experience such grief once again? Anger was pulsing through her veins and she held nothing back.

As she sat there, she heard a voice say: "My child, why are you so angry with me?" She was initially unsure whether she had really God's voice or whether it was just her mind playing tricks. Then she heard the voice again, and this time God said: "I allowed you to hold one of my angels in your arms today."

Bridie was stunned. A sense of peace washed over her and all her anger evaporated. She felt completely different all of a sudden; so full of the Lord's comfort. She saw it as a privilege to have been there with the little boy rather than an ordeal. She felt blessed that she been able to hold his little body close so he would have known warmth and love through human contact during his last minutes on earth.

Unbeknown to her, Mick was at the prayer meeting she had refused to go to, asking the Lord to bring his wife peace. He was aware that he couldn't have done what he was doing without her, and that he would have been useless without this wise wee wummin by his side.

The days and weeks rolled into years, and the couple threw themselves wholeheartedly into sharing practical and emotional love wherever they went. Every time they needed something the Lord provided, most often through the generosity of others but sometimes though divine intervention as far as Bridie was concerned.

There was so much disease and infection around they were warned by interpreters and church leaders to wear masks and keep their distance from people, but Mick always hugged everyone he met, offering the love of Christ indiscriminately. He argued that Jesus had walked among the poor and so would he. He really demonstrated the love of God to these people. He had all the time in the world for them, and would just light up people's lives with his big infectious smile and those beautiful blue eyes of his. They saw lice jumping off people's heads everywhere they went, yet somehow Mick and Bridie never caught them.

This new sense of purpose gave the couple fresh hope to cling to as they went about the business of raising much-needed cash for the impoverished Romanian people. Tom proved to be a great friend to them both, and Mick and Tom forged a friendship that ran deeper than most. They became like family and worked incredibly well together, chatting for hours and hours on their long trips. They were convinced this was the work the Lord was asking them to do, and both felt real joy at giving the families they met an opportunity to eat, stay warm and have a roof over their heads.

Mick was such a committed, big-hearted man, but sometimes he frustrated Tom a little. They had a set amount of cash to give each family, and Tom felt it was important that everyone received the same amount so there could be no fighting or jealousy. But every now and again he would look back as they were leaving a family to see Mick shaking hands with someone, and he would just know that Mick had given them a wee bit extra. Whenever Tom said anything, Mick would just smile and say their need had been particularly desperate.

Bridie was also fond of Tom, and was delighted they had all bonded, but especially the two men, who had to travel so much and for such long periods. She was impressed to see that a cross word never passed between them. The passion they all had for helping the poor was contagious, and back at home they continued to set up more sponsorship arrangements and spread the word about what they were doing. Just £40 a month from a family in Northern Ireland made a massive difference to a family in Romania and really had the power to change lives. The people who agreed to sponsor families never once asked for details of where their money was going, trusting that the charity's leaders were being guided by God to do what was right, and holding Mick and Bridie in the highest esteem.

The sponsorship idea had been birthed in Romania when an old lady was so desperate she clung to Mick, begging him to help pay her rent as she was about to be evicted. Mick gave her the money but was immediately told off by the housekeeper, who insisted he shouldn't have done so as the charity couldn't give everyone money and she felt it would encourage more people to ask for it. Mick looked directly at the housekeeper and said: "We can bring all the clothes and goods in the world over here, but these people need money too, and I know my Lord Jesus wants me to give what I can." She didn't argue with that!

There were tough times on these trips, but there was also a great deal of laughter along the way. On one occasion they had their very own 'Pretty Woman' experience. An elderly lady was looking longingly through a shop window, dreaming of buying some of the food and clothes inside but not being anywhere close to being able to afford it. The shopkeeper came out and shooed her away several times, letting her know she wasn't wanted anywhere near his premises.

This lady, whom Mick and Bridie personally decided to sponsor, went back to the shop another day, and the owner who had previously chased her away started fawning all over her, aware that the McGoldricks had given her some money. However, the lovely old lady started holding her nose and making faces as if there were a bad smell in the shop, then asked Mick and Bridie to take her out immediately. They all laughed so hard about the disgruntled shopkeeper's face as the three of them left abruptly in mock disgust.

Bridie couldn't help but laugh on another occasion after meeting a young lady who had the worst squint she had ever seen.

The Glaswegian woman's heart was so touched she went off to find out how much it would cost to fix. The people living in the area told her it would need to be done in Bucharest at a cost of around £200. Bridie told Mick she wanted to pay for the woman to get it done and would repay the money from her own pocket when they got home. Mick agreed, and they gave the woman the money.

Sometime later the girl tapped Bridie on the shoulder and pointed to her eye. She looked truly fantastic and expressed her total delight at the change. Days later, however, they discovered she hadn't had an operation at all. It had been a glass eye all along, and the woman had simply turned it around the wrong way to win their sympathy. Thankfully, Bridie saw the funny side, understanding that desperate times often called for desperate measures!

Another time the couple paid for an operation on behalf of a young man who had a terrible limp following a really nasty leg break. Mick had arranged for him to be treated and the damage was fixed. About a year later, while Mick was shaving one morning, a knock came at the door. Mick answered it to find the same young guy he had helped standing there. He was pleading for help once again, asking Mick to intervene as he had had another medical condition. Mick didn't understand everything the lad was saying, but when he pointed to the doctor's letter, which stated that he had venereal disease, Mick chased him away. He said to Bridie later that day: "I got his leg fixed so he could get a job and a leg up, not so he could get his leg over!" The pair of them doubled over with laughter at the brazenness of the poor guy.

When Bridie wasn't able to travel with them, Tom and Mick would regale her with tales from their long journeys across Europe in their van, packed to the gunnels with all the provisions they could muster. Often during these trips they were saved from harm by a kind stranger or an unusually helpful official at just the right moment. It was obvious to them all that God was blessing this ministry and opening doors for them to go and love the people of Romania in his name. It also became clear that the ones he was leading them to were the poorest, dirtiest, smelliest people, who were every bit as precious and valuable in his eyes as anyone else. That selfless love for the least and the forgotten burned as brightly within Bridie as it had back in the Gorbals, where she had also been committed to fighting injustice and helping the oppressed.

Tom fondly remembers Mick's big-hearted generosity, but there was a different side to his character that surfaced when the occasion demanded. Mick was a great advocate for the downtrodden, loving those he encountered like Jesus, but he wasn't intimidated by anyone. One time he saw a burly man go into a woman's house immediately after they had given her some goods and money. He knew she was alone, as her husband was in prison, and he sensed something wasn't right. Sure enough, they made it back inside just in time to see this big guy threatening the woman with violence if she refused to hand over everything Mick and Tom had just given her. She was clearly terrified.

Not caring a jot about the size or strength difference, Mick grabbed the man and threw him out. He fiercely stood his ground, and despite being huge the guy backed down and walked away. People soon learned that Mick was no shrinking violet when it came to battling injustice.

One thing that always delighted Bridie was seeing the hand of God undeniably at work in an impossible situation. One particular time Mick sat down and worked out that they had enough money to help ninety-five families. They had travelled to a new area of Romania and felt God was leading them to a specific village. Not knowing how to help, the couple went to see the parish priest, whom they had never met before. He told them it was a small, desperate community comprising ninety-five families! They were both delighted and a little overwhelmed that God had led them there so intentionally.

Life was full of change, and things were moving along rapidly for United Christian Aid. Romania was about to join the EU, and the team knew that life would improve for the country's inhabitants as a result. They all felt it was time to shift the charity's focus elsewhere and seek new folks to help. They asked God to direct them to the next place he wanted them to go. After plenty of prayer and seeking God, it became clear that he was sending them to Moldova. Bridie, Mick and Tom were all in agreement that this was where God was calling them to, and it wasn't long before they were taking the practical love of God into this small European country full of hurting and broken people. Tom and Mick replicated what they had done in Romania and soon established United Christian Aid in Moldova. The two men felt privileged to be bringing the love of Christ to the poorest of the poor in very practical ways.

The sights the couple saw there were similar to those they had faced for the past seven years, if not worse. Mick proved to be Bridie's inspiration as well as her best friend as they travelled around the country together. As before, they had to overcome a fair amount of prejudice and mistrust from the people there, but once again Mick went straight ahead and loved people in the name of Jesus. He just opened his arms and hugged everyone he met. He soon won the trust of whole villages, where the people were often desperate to simply be noticed. The fact that the McGoldricks placed no conditions or requirements on their giving spoke volumes to the poor and overlooked. The couple's faith in the Almighty to provide was always rewarded as they trusted him to meet the many needs they saw around them.

Mick was particularly aware of the plight of women in Eastern Europe, recognising how much they had suffered under communism. He always marvelled at the way the mothers in these desperately poor families kept everything together. Often there was no running water in their homes, if they even had homes, yet they kept their children as clean as possible and looked after their meagre belongings, in addition to holding down jobs and looking after elderly family members.

With their usual love and commitment, the couple signed up sponsors and gathered food, clothes and household goods for the people of this forgotten land. Communities in Northern Ireland continued to embrace the work of the charity and were always keen to hear from them, either through their speaking engagements or via the familiar United Christian Aid van Mick and Tom travelled around in to collect the donations. Mick was loved and admired by young and old alike, and the number of kettles that just happened to have been put on before he arrived was enough to wipe out the national grid! Not only did he show the love of Christ to the broken and needy in Moldova, but he was also like a magnet for folks in his local area. Mick McGoldrick was a blessing wherever he went.

One time a wealthy young lady got in touch to say she was considering donating her wedding present money to charity. She met with Mick and Bridie and asked a series of questions but never committed the cash to United Christian Aid. She said she planned to split her money between several charities, then thanked them for their time and left. They put it out of their minds and time passed by.

Mick was away in Moldova when the young lady phoned to say she would be giving them the full amount as she couldn't get past the impression Mick had made. She said that he was the most unselfish man she had ever met, which made Bridie laugh as she had so often said the same thing. As the call was winding up, she asked whether Bridie wanted to know the amount. It turned out she was giving them a cheque for £20,000!

Bridie was ecstatic and immediately called Mick. She eventually got through and told him the news, but the line immediately went dead. She called and called but couldn't get through again. It was two in the morning by the time Bridie went to bed, and she still didn't know whether Mick had heard what she had said. They finally connected the following day, and he told her that right at the moment when she had called he had been standing with 100 families but had nothing to give them aside from hugs. The money the woman was donating would mean the entire village could be sponsored for two years!

God was at work in the lives of many people to bring about his will at this time, both at home and abroad. Mick and Tom often found themselves in situations where they didn't have the relevant paperwork the officials who stopped them were looking for, yet they seemed to overcome every hurdle without issue. Moldova was still a difficult place to reach, and people there were severely lacking in basic necessities, yet it became a second home for the staff of United Christian Aid, and Mick was a beloved adopted son among the people there.

Tom was well aware that they were never alone on any of the trips they went on. He saw Jesus working so clearly through his friend and travelling companion, who embodied the Saviour's love, grace and acceptance. One day as they were walking along the street, Mick turned and said, "Tom, it's as if Jesus is walking these streets with us.

I can feel him so close." And so could those they visited, as time after time they arrived at exactly the right moment with exactly the right items to meet the people's needs. They were also able to reach people in ways that bigger organisations couldn't, as the two directors were right there together, distributing the goods and God's love, and were able to make executive decisions on the spot.

Mick and Tom were as committed to helping the Moldovans as they had been with the Romanians and were tireless in their efforts, always pushing themselves to the limit with just one more house to visit or one final hug to give. The folks they met were always enamoured with the strange accents and loving hugs of Mr Mick and Mr Tom. And as it turned out, life was also getting busier for the McGoldricks on home soil.

CHAPTER 18:
Speaking Up

God was bringing more and more speaking engagements into the McGoldricks' lives back in Ireland, and their remarkable story of forgiveness continued to be an inspiration to many. The extent of their pain could never be fully understood by those listening, yet the depth of their love for God and his Son burned brightly. The reality of life without Michael, however purpose-filled, had left scars that wouldn't heal this side of heaven, but their trademark humour and honesty stood the couple in great stead as they travelled around sharing their story.

All Mick wanted was to get the truth out there that there was a God who loved everyone – a God who had sent his own Son to die on the cross for them – and that he loved every man, woman and child. He always had a twinkle in his eyes when he spoke, and people instantly warmed to him. Part of the couple's charm as they shared with others was that they weren't trained speakers or professionals. They were just an ordinary husband and wife who were speaking from the heart. It didn't matter where they went; their honest and open approach was always the same.

Someone who fully understood the McGoldricks' pain was Joan Wilson, whose daughter Marie had been murdered in the IRA Poppy Day bombing in Enniskillen. She was just twenty years old at the time and had gone there with her father, Joan's husband Gordon, who survived the attack. Like Bridie and Mick, the Wilsons had a strong faith, and Gordon had said publicly that he bore his daughter's killers no ill will. Joan and Gordon travelled around Northern Ireland speaking about peace and reconciliation for years. Sadly, the couple's second child, Peter, died suddenly in a car accident and Gordon himself passed away just six months later in 1995. Bridie had the utmost respect for Joan, whom she described as a very dignified lady, and the unimaginable horror the two women had endured created a deep bond that few others will thankfully ever share.

Someone else who had been impressed and inspired by the McGoldricks was none other than American senator Edward "Ted" Kennedy, brother of John F. Kennedy. Ted happened to be speaking at an event related to the peace process in Derry in 1998. It was a cause dear to his heart due to his Irish roots, and he wanted Mick and Bridie to come along. The pair had no idea how powerful their courageous story was or how much of an impact it was making, but Senator Kennedy had heard about the couple and wanted to thank them personally for the difference they were making. At first Bridie didn't believe it was really the senator who had called, struggling to accept that anyone so important would be calling them. Mick was as surprised and baffled as Bridie to receive the call, but they were both completely bowled over all the same.

The day finally came and the couple travelled to Derry together. They were chauffeur-driven to a hotel that had been taken over for the event. When the pair arrived they met Irish politician John Hume and his wife Patricia, who were warm, welcoming and helped them feel more relaxed. Again, the McGoldricks were astonished that the Humes even knew who they were.

This grand event saw Mick take to the stage to speak alongside Senator Kennedy. The McGoldricks waited outside the room before entering, not wanting to walk on the red carpet that had been laid out for the visiting dignitaries. It wasn't until someone pointed out they were, in fact, among those dignitaries that they dared step on it! Mick may have been speaking to, and alongside, some of the most powerful and influential people in the world, but he took to the stage with his usual humility and honesty, wrapped up in the compassion that always drove him to share his faith. Many lives were touched that night.

They were introduced to Ted Kennedy later in the day. Bridie hadn't expected him to make such a great impression on them, but he was a massive man and extremely charismatic. She quickly felt completely at ease and enjoyed his company. He had obviously been well briefed, as he knew a huge amount about them; much more than they knew about him. The senator thanked them for all the good they had done in helping to further the peace process. He said their story had really touched him, and that he admired their strength and courage. It was such a natural conversation, yet it also felt completely surreal.

They talked at length about Michael and what a great boy he had been, and Ted was able to empathise, given that two of his brothers had been shot and killed. John F. Kennedy had famously been assassinated in an open-top car in November 1963 while he was President of the United States . Robert Kennedy, a US senator in Los Angeles, who had been widely tipped to become president, was murdered five years later. Ted also knew the heartache of seeing a child suffer, as his son had been diagnosed with bone cancer, which led to his leg being amputated.

Another special guest at the Derry event was Jean Kennedy Smith, Ted's sister and the US Ambassador to Ireland under Bill Clinton's administration. She had been instrumental in bringing Ted over to Ireland and was widely lauded for playing a major part in facilitating talks during the peace process.

The conversation flowed as the McGoldricks swapped stories with Ted and Jean. Imposing and captivating, Ted Kennedy may have been one of the most influential men in American politics at the time, coming as he did from a dynasty of political and presidential leaders and having his own successful campaigns to boot, but while he was in the presence of this humble yet wise couple from the university of life, he was regaled with funny tales, given plenty of good advice and blessed with a healthy dollop of straight talk.

Jean certainly impressed Bridie, who deemed her a "real lady". She spoke with the couple at length, and not only was she just as warm and welcoming as Ted had been, but she was just as knowledgeable about their story. Bridie and Mick were extremely impressed by her obvious commitment to helping their country find peace. At the end of the night she refused to get into her waiting car, despite the fact it was pouring with rain, until she saw that transport had been arranged for them. Instead, she stood and chatted until Mick and Bridie got into their taxi. Despite having met countless people over the years, it seemed as though this humble couple made a particularly lasting impression on the international ambassador.

Life wasn't all red carpets and fancy dresses, however. Mick and Bridie were still immersed in the work they were doing across Eastern Europe and spent most days gathering goods to transport there or encouraging Irish families to sponsor their Eastern European counterparts. The couple's lovely home doubled as a hub for the whole organisation, and it was always filled with goods and visitors.

The whole family was supportive of their work, and Jacqueline was among those who saw the impact it was having on many people's lives. Once again, she was inspired by her hard-working and selfless aunty and uncle, and impressed by the way they were able to put their own pain and anguish to one side to help as many other people as possible.

Life at home was settling into a new and familiar pattern for the couple. They were still constantly mourning the loss of Michael, but were also receiving the strength they needed from their deeper relationship with God. They were keen to draw close to their heavenly Father at Mass every morning to lay their burden of pain at the cross. They had been able to forgive Michael's killer, yet they needed the daily grace and mercy God bestowed on them to push through the agony.

Once again, spending time with their family and friends was a source of great pleasure for the couple, and their willingness to look after Andrew continued to be a blessing for Sadie. Bridie was continually impressed by her hard-working daughter-in-law, who was doing all she could to keep her little family together. The days and nights were so lonely for Sadie without her soulmate, and Bridie and Mick did everything they could to ease her pain. Andrew was such a little character and he came along to Mass with them, charming the priests and parishioners there. He was a happy, chatty boy, and he certainly kept Mick and Bridie on their toes. Mick spent hours playing football with and reading to Andrew, reminding Bridie of Mick and Michael's relationship all those years earlier.

Although it was a bittersweet time, spending precious hours with Michael's son was a wonderful tonic for Bridie, and she relished her role in the young boy's life. Emma was also doted on, and Bridie loved buying her pretty dresses and outfits, as well as coordinating shoes and hats. This was also bittersweet, as it broke Bridie's heart to see Emma looking so beautiful or coming home with another glowing school report and not to have her daddy there to hug her. She did well at school from an early age, and it was lovely for the couple to play such an important part in the little girl's life. They were able to encourage, listen and be there for her when the void of her daddy's death became too much. It was incredibly hard that Michael couldn't be there to watch her grow, but Bridie knew her son would have been so proud of his little princess.

The shadow of Michael's death never went away, and in 2001 a man named Clifford McKeown was arrested and detained on suspicion of his murder. Journalist Nick Martin Clark had inadvertently found out from Clifford that he had murdered Michael while interviewing him about something else. Despite the great personal cost, both professionally and personally, Nick Martin Clark went straight to the police.

At the height of the Drumcree standoff during that fateful summer of 1996, loyalist paramilitary organisation the Ulster Volunteer Force (UVF), had an infamous member called Billy Wright, known to his peers as "King Rat". There had reportedly been a plan to kidnap three local priests and kill two of them, but fearing this would provoke reprisals against Protestant clergy the group had aborted its plans. However, McKeown had decided to carry out an atrocity anyway. He plotted and carried out Michael's senseless killing as a birthday present for Billy Wright. Incidentally, Billy Wright was murdered himself by members of the Irish National Liberation Army (INLA) in 1999, although many believe they had some inside assistance, as Wright was in a maximum-security prison at the time.

There were allegedly two young accomplices with McKeown on the night of Michael's murder, who had ordered a taxi in the name of Lavery. They asked Michael to take them up the lonely Aghagallon Lane and pretended they needed to stop to urinate. Then McKeown, who had been following behind them in his car with the lights out, shot Michael five times in the back of the head while he sat at the wheel of his taxi.

Bridie and Mick stayed away from the trial, but Sadie went every day. In 2003, some seven years after the brutal slaying, Clifford McKeown was sentenced to twenty-four years in prison. The couple were hounded by the press again when McKeown was found guilty and sentenced, as everyone was keen to find out whether their forgiveness was still intact once they had been able to put a name and face to their son's murderer.

Their reply never changed one iota, however, though they were still only able to forgive by the grace of God. They weren't superhuman, and their hearts were unquestionably broken, but they both knew God was asking them to forgive others as he had forgiven them. This resolute bravery and commitment to love others as God loved ran through Bridie like the letters through a stick of rock. Thrust onto a platform she never chose or wanted, she remains as full of grace today as she was back then.

Not everyone was able to be so forgiving, however. Jacqueline struggled at times to deal with the pain the trial brought with it, and she felt extremely angry when all the details came out. It was harrowing for family and friends to hear what had really happened to Michael, especially as Jacqueline had seen the damage it had done to Mick and Bridie up close. The young woman admired their strength and their choice to forgive, but it was hard for her to come to terms with it all.

The pain of hearing the cold, cruel facts of Michael's murder is still etched into Bridie's face today. She faces daily battles to stop her mind wandering into those dark, desperate places of the imagination, but whatever evil has been done to her, God's goodness and grace have overcome it.

Although Mick and Bridie hadn't managed to get away together for several years, Bridie was as content as she could be with the way life was going. The pair were busy speaking at various church gatherings across Ireland, inspiring those who heard their story and who saw the compassion and love for others in their eyes. Life may not have been a bed of roses, but Bridie felt completely secure in her faith and her marriage. She was immersed in the work of the charity and still madly in love with the blue-eyed wonder by her side. God and her darling Mick had helped her put the pieces of her broken heart back together, but sadly this settled phase wasn't to last forever.

CHAPTER 19:
No, No, No!

Mick and Bridie were up preparing for Mick's 3.30am departure to Moldova on the morning of 30th March 2006. Bridie busied herself packing up the usual treats – boiled eggs and his favourite biscuits – for the journey and making sure he had all he needed. Mick always looked forward to going out, although he looked forward to coming back to his wife even more. When everything was ready, Bridie said, "God bless. Keep safe and I love you." Mick told her how much he loved her in return and then off he went.

Bridie waited up to hear that Mick had arrived safely, then put her head down to get some sleep. On the Saturday night he called to say he was in agony with stomach pains, which they both thought was a bad case of constipation; something he often suffered with. Bridie wasn't overly concerned, but felt slightly annoyed when he didn't call later that night as they had arranged. Nevertheless, she put it out of her mind, assuming he had got himself caught up in the mission and simply forgotten.

A few hours later, Tom called her to say they had visited a local hospital and the medical staff had decided to keep Mick in for observation as he was in such a lot of pain. Again, Bridie wasn't unduly concerned, still thinking it was constipation, and she went up to the chapel hall as usual. Tom wasn't desperately worried for his friend either, especially as Mick had insisted that Tom go and distribute money to the villagers as planned, confident that he would be fine. When Tom visited him in hospital later, however, he was surprised when they decided to keep Mick in overnight. His condition had taken a turn for the worse, and Tom realised the situation might be more serious than he had first thought.

On Bridie's return from chapel she received a call from Tom to say that Mick was being taken into theatre the following day and that the medical staff were concerned. Bridie called Father Tom and went next door to tell Maura. Father Tom, Sadie and Maura all came over to sit with her.

Bridie called Tom so she could speak to Mick before he went down to theatre. She told Tom he must go to the hospital, head right into theatre if necessary and tell them she had to speak to Mick before they started the operation. Tom argued at first, saying it wouldn't be possible, but Bridie was adamant, practically ordering him to get Mick on the phone. Favour or fear prevailed, and she was connected with her husband just as he was going in. She was so glad to hear his voice, especially when he said, "Oh, sweetheart, when I'm back on my feet we're going on holiday!"

Bridie told him she was heading out to Moldova right away, but he told her not to come. He said the journey would kill her, given her poor health, and that he couldn't live without her. He added that she was his rock and told her he loved her. She told him she loved him right back, the exact words they had both said to Michael the last time they spoke to him. Mick was then wheeled into surgery while Bridie sat and waited. And waited.

Tom called later that day and spoke with Sadie and Father Tom. Bridie hadn't known about the call until the two of them came to break the news that her beloved Mick had never regained consciousness and had died on the operating table. Mick McGoldrick died of septicaemia brought on by a bleeding abscess on 3rd April 3

2006 at the age of sixty-four, just three months short of the tenth anniversary of Michael's murder.

Once again, Bridie was plunged into a world of grief and disbelief, only this time her rock and soulmate wasn't there to hold her hand or comfort her. Barely able to function, she felt completely bereft. She ran into the toilet and locked the door on hearing the news. She was completely overcome and just couldn't take it in.

The house was soon filled with people, but Bridie could hardly speak. She didn't want anyone around her except the one person she couldn't have, her darling Mick. Bridie was in a daze, as though she were surrounded by fog. She was aware that Father Tom was saying prayers but couldn't believe what was happening. In total shock, she simply couldn't accept that her Mick was gone. It was just too cruel.

The next morning an emptiness poured over her, flooding her to the core with hopelessness and despair. Bridie took Sadie by the arm and told her there was only one thing that mattered to her at that moment, and that she would sell their home to make it happen if necessary. She just wanted his body back with her. She wanted her Mick home.

Unfortunately, this wasn't a simple thing to accomplish. Because United Christian Aid's staff willingly went into danger zones the charity had been unable to acquire insurance cover, so Bridie was facing astronomical costs as well as lengthy delays. Bringing her beloved husband home would be no easy feat. She had no idea how much it would cost or how to go about it, but she desperately needed to have him home with her as quickly as possible. She needed to see him, to hold him.

Bridie faced a daunting wait to see if and how she could make it happen. In a country ravaged by communism and poverty, the amount of red tape and corruption she encountered was overwhelming. It seemed likely that it could take up to six months for Mick's body to be brought home.

As usual, she wasn't left alone in her plight. The entire community rallied around, starting with their much-loved parish priest. Father Tom came to her with £5,000 he had been saving up for the couple. He knew they hadn't been on holiday for a long time and had wanted to surprise them. He apologised for giving her the money for this purpose, but said that he hoped it would help to bring Mick's body back.

Surrounded by chaos, Bridie felt engulfed by grief and shock, but fortunately her nearest and dearest were always by her side. Sadie was an amazing support throughout. She made phone calls and carried out endless research in an attempt to make things happen. Bridie could focus on nothing else; she just needed to see her Mick and get him home. She wanted to go out there and make it happen herself, but given her frail health and the travel restrictions in Moldova it didn't seem like a good idea.

Bridie's family and friends were understandably worried about her. The news of Mick's death had been completely devastating, and the fact she was having to jump through relentless administration hoops simply added to the pain. Christina clearly remembers the shock and disbelief that gripped her precious family at this bleak time. She couldn't imagine what Bridie must be going through, having lost her son and then her soulmate. She had truly adored him, and he had been so in love with her all those years. Like everyone else who knew and loved them, Christina was totally stunned that he was gone.

Jacqueline was also in shock and disbelief.. Mick had been like a father to her, and she was devastated by the loss of the man she had known and loved nearly all her adult life. She had been on a boat coming back from Scotland when she received the call to say that Mick was going in for the operation. Her son Martin was with her at the time, and they knew it didn't sound good. It was such a shock, in fact, that Jacqueline felt a panic attack coming on. They hoped and hoped he would pull through, but a family friend was there to meet them when they got off the boat and told them the news they had been dreading. Jacqueline simply couldn't believe it. The first thing they did was go to be with Bridie. The house was full of people, but Bridie was so lost again, and Jacqueline's heart went out to her. It just seemed so unfair.

It was a bitter blow for Martin as well, given how much he loved the man who had treated him like a grandson all his life. Sadness engulfed him, but he knew he needed to go and support his adopted aunt. It seemed especially cruel to Martin that Mick had died out in Moldova, so far from home and his beloved wife. Like everyone else, he was concerned that she would struggle to cope with such a great loss again. He was heartbroken, shattered by the realisation that they would never see Mick again. It felt so unfair that Bridie had lost her whole family, especially as both Mick and Michael had meant the world to her.

Someone else who was devastated by the news of Mick's death was Father Charles, a young priest from Malawi who had entered Mick and Bridie's life during the winter of 2004. He had come to stay for two days en route to starting his studies in Dublin but had loved being with Mick and Bridie so much that he had been with them as much as possible during the two years leading up to Mick's death, even calling them Mum and Dad.

The news of Mick's death was almost unbearable for Father Charles, but he was really there for Bridie at this terrible time. He gradually helped her accept that God had not been cruel to her in letting Mick die so far away. He had prayed about it and believed God had said that Mick needed to die in Moldova so the people there didn't think he had just abandoned them and stopped coming to help through his own choice. The fact he had died while serving them was a real blessing for the Moldovans. He said that it wasn't a random accident. The hand of the Almighty had been working things for good, even at such a terrible time. This thought continues to comfort her today.

Bridie was slowly coming to terms with her situation and knew she would have to start arranging the funeral, even though the body still hadn't been released. Father Tom McAteer had always been close to Mick, so Bridie wanted him to be involved. Three other priests had offered to say the Mass, such was the popularity of the humble man who had loved people the way Jesus had every step of his way. Bridie received calls from all around the world from people who were keen to pass on their condolences and extend offers of help. She was grateful afterwards, but at the time she was still adrift in a sea of grief and barely aware of what was happening around her.

One day, the former Moderator of the General Assembly of the Presbyterian Church in Ireland, Ken Newell, called to pass on his condolences and offer Bridie his services, offering to do anything he could to help. He said that the world had lost a great man and asked

Bridie to allow him to participate in Mick's funeral, such was his admiration for Mick. Bridie agreed, although she was still too numb to take everything in.

Despite everyone's kindness, Bridie couldn't find any comfort. All she could focus on was getting Mick home. Progress was finally made after much prayer and petitioning. In addition to the family, local priests, politicians and even members of local paramilitary groups who had been deeply impressed by the dignity and humility of Mick's life offered their assistance in an attempt to bring Mick back from Moldova.

The weight of expectation hung heavily on Tom's shoulders as he tried to ensure that Mick's body was brought home amid dealing with his own shock and pain at what had happened. It was a nightmare trying to get things organised with so much red tape and everything being done through interpreters. He knew how desperate Bridie was to have her husband's body home and did everything he could to make it happen as quickly as possible.

Across Moldova, the poorest of the poor were organising petitions and pleading with officials to send Mr Mick back to the UK. Their cause was heard, and it was miraculously arranged that Mick's body would be brought home in just six days using Tom's passport rather than the predicted six months. Thousands of people lined the streets to say goodbye. They threw flowers onto his coffin, a simple wooden box, as it passed through the streets and villages on the way to the capital. The coffin had to stop at every village because everyone was so upset by his death.

Tom watched in humble admiration as old widows and widowers gave their last pennies, everything they had, because the whole country was so determined to get him home to his wife. He had known Mick was loved prior to his untimely death, but it was still really touching for him to see just how deep that love ran. Bridie was also deeply touched by this display of earnest, costly generosity when Tom told her about it sometime later.

Back at home, Sadie was giving Bridie sedatives with her cups of tea, as she was really worried about the effects of all the stress on her mother-in-law's heart. The tablets kept Bridie calm but made her feel remote from the situation, as though she were just an onlooker.

She hadn't eaten or slept since receiving that fateful phone call several days earlier. The family knew that seeing Mick's body would make it feel real, but it was all Bridie could think about.

Bridie had no idea how much it cost, but all the arrangements were finally taken care of. And so, draped in the Moldovan flag as he made the journey from Dublin to County Armagh, Mick came home on the Sunday morning after his death. Her darling husband had come home for the last time. The grief Bridie felt when his body came through the door was overwhelming. She could see her soulmate lying there, yet it still didn't seem real.

Sadie, Jacqueline, Father Tom, Margaret, John and a whole host of other friends and family members were there for Bridie around the clock. Once again, the house was filled to the rafters with every kind of sandwich and cake imaginable, as friends and even strangers ached to do anything they could for this grief-stricken woman. But although she knew how much everyone cared, and appreciated that her husband had elicited such a widespread display of grief, Bridie desperately wanted to shut the doors so she could simply be with her beloved husband.

The coffin was laid on top of their bed and droves of people poured in to pay their respects. During the day he belonged to the people, but at night he was all hers. She would lie beside Mick on the bed just to be close to him. He had always said that he wanted to lie in his own bed before he was buried, and that's exactly what he did, albeit inside the coffin. He looked so handsome to his grieving wife. At one point she even put his glasses on his face in the hope that his beautiful blue eyes would open.

Christina came over from Scotland to be with her beloved aunt, and although she had known how awesome Mick was, it still impressed her to see how many people from all walks of life came to pay their respects. It really touched her to see the house packed full of friends, neighbours, bishops, priests, nuns, politicians and many others. But to Christina he was just her Uncle Mick; the man who had been there all her life with his loving smile and wise words. It was impossible to believe he was gone, but it helped to see people reaching out. Having done so much good and helping so many people, it was quite special to see that come back around when Bridie needed it. It made Christina realise that helping others really mattered.

Bridie had no idea that television channels, radio stations and newspapers from all over the world had been covering the story, and once again they were all scrambling for quotes and photos. Her softly spoken, uncomplicated husband may not have been one for the limelight, but his passing was recognised as a bitter blow to the peace process and to the whole community in Northern Ireland.

Such was the esteem in which Mick had been held that local paramilitary groups came to the house to say that their flags would be flying at half mast as a mark of respect. It seemed inconceivable that one man, and especially someone without the platform of election or celebrity, could evoke such heartfelt and widespread admiration. It might have been disconcerting for some to see opposing members of major paramilitary groups having a cup of tea in Bridie's lounge as they came to pay their respects, but it was further testimony to the unifying presence Mick McGoldrick had, and proof that even in death his message of love was more powerful than the deep-rooted hatred around them.

Not everyone who came to pay their respects was genuine, however. In the midst of their grief, in walked a man Bridie had never seen before. Many people who had met Mick as he collected for the charity or travelled abroad had appeared at the house, so at first nobody paid much attention. The family made him several plates of sandwiches and cakes along with plenty of cups of tea before Bridie started to get suspicious. He couldn't answer any questions about how he knew Mick, so some of the relatives asked him to leave but he wouldn't go. He just kept asking for more food and saying, "An angel has left the earth. An angel has left the earth." They eventually worked out that he didn't know Mick or Bridie at all, and was actually a professional mourner who simply went to local wakes to get fed and watered.

Mick's death was a harrowing, shocking event for all those who had known him, and Bridie felt as though she couldn't carry on. She just wanted to go to be with her boys. The whole family was reeling from the sudden loss and afraid for Bridie as she mourned the death of her soulmate. Thankfully, her family was right there for her throughout, supporting her, loving her and helping her get the funeral service arranged. Margaret and John barely left her side, while Sadie, strong as always, attended to many of the practical things that needed doing. Nevertheless, cardinals and bishops joined the throng at the house, along with friends from the local bingo hall, where she and Mick had been regulars, and many of the couple's Christian brothers and sisters. This would be no ordinary funeral because Mick had been no ordinary man.

Bridie wanted to involve as many people as possible in the funeral service. She knew various television and radio reporters would be there, although she had no idea at the time that it would garner global interest. The phone was ringing off the hook once again, but she hardly knew a thing about it, as those around her were so brilliant at handling everything. All Bridie could focus on was the fact that her Mick was lying on their bed in a coffin. She couldn't even begin to process it.

Although it's still raw and painful to think about, a smile is never far from Bridie's face when she thinks about the man who shared her heart and life for so long. This is especially true when she thinks about an embarrassing incident that took place just before the funeral. The coffin had been decorated by the people of Moldova, and a beautiful, intricate lace cover had been made by some Orthodox nuns. The work they had put into it was outstanding, and many people commented on it.

A few Christmases earlier, Bridie had found the perfect present for her fun-loving husband. She had bought a pair of pink fluffy handcuffs as a joke and given them to Mick, who had promptly fallen to the floor laughing, tears flowing, and saying that Bridie never ceased to amaze him. As they prepared for the funeral, Bridie remembered them and told Sadie she wanted to put them inside the coffin with him as a wee token of the humour they had shared, and of how their physical desire for one another had never waned. In fact, the twinkle in Mick's eyes had been reserved for Bridie alone in the bedroom. The handcuffs were discreetly placed under a cover in the coffin and duly forgotten about.

The day before the funeral, the room was filled with bishops, nuns, priests and ministers, all of whom had gathered to pray and pay their respects. As they mourned and ministered, one of the nuns standing at the top end of the coffin quietly asked another nun if she knew what was to happen with the beautiful lace cover that had been draped over the outside. From nowhere, Andrew's little voice piped up: "It's going into the coffin beside Gran and Grandpa's pink handcuffs."

Bridie nearly died of embarrassment. She whispered softly to Sadie that she hoped the nuns were deaf. The priest standing next to her at the time said: "They might be, but I'm not." Bridie's face turned almost as pink as the handcuffs!

However, laughter was in short supply the Thursday after Mick's body was returned home as the family made their way to the chapel to lay him to rest. Bridie was distraught and found herself saying the hardest prayer she had ever prayed as she did the rosary for Mick. She felt distraught and also a little angry with Mick for leaving her behind.

This courageous woman, who had already faced enormous heartache, had to gather all her faith and strength as she fought through her darkest thoughts and feelings. However much she wanted to delay it, the time had come for her to let them take Mick away and be buried beside his precious boy. She had faced intense pain before, but had always had her other half beside her. Never had two people been more heartbroken or more united as they had been after Michael's death; so down, yet so there for each other. This couple had been rescued from suicide by their faith in God, and Bridie knew that only the Almighty could pull her through at this moment.

Doubting she would be able to cope, Bridie straightened her back, squared her shoulders and held her head high as she looked over at her husband's coffin. She was determined to give Mick McGoldrick the best send-off she could muster. And that's exactly what she did.

Andrew led his 'papa' out of the house, then received him at the chapel. Father Tom led the service, with readings from Emma and Ken Newell. Andrew served the Mass, while Sadie sang the final hymn, "Be Not Afraid". This delighted Bridie, as her daughter-in-law had such a beautiful voice and it seemed fitting that Sadie had such a pivotal part to play, having been a rock to her mother-in-law throughout. The words of this hymn were especially poignant, given that a big part of Mick's life had been spent bringing relief and aid to the poorest of the poor.

The whole funeral embodied Mick's faith as well as his amazing love for everyone he met, regardless of age, gender or status. It was fitting that this spiritual giant was honoured for the love, generosity and goodness he had shared with others throughout his life.

Martin had been asked to help carry the coffin from the chapel to the grave. Initially he hadn't wanted to, thinking it would be too difficult, but his family managed to persuade him, and looking back he is glad to have had such an honour bestowed on him. He was still heartbroken, however, as they had all loved Mick so much, and his vision was blurred with tears as he fulfilled this important duty. And so this humble man was carried to his eternal rest on the shoulders of the family and friends who knew and loved him best, then laid beside the earthly remains of his beloved son.

Sometimes Bridie will still say to him: "Mick, I'm jealous you're with our boy but I still can't see him." She is absolutely positive they'll be kicking a ball about in heaven. Comforted by the fact that they will be happy together, she still misses them both terribly and is desperate to be with them. But while desperation may have engulfed her at times, Bridie wasn't even able to consider suicide this time round. Her faith had grown so much and she knew the Lord still had a plan for her, even if she couldn't see it at the time.

Mick was gone and her heart was truly broken. Surrounded by well-wishers, Bridie came home from the funeral in ongoing shock, but the day had brought with it a heartbreaking closure. With the house still filled with loving friends and family members, she slept properly for the first time since Mick's death. The exhaustion and grief too terrible to bear, she was completely out for the count.

People were there, day and night, to look after her, make cups of tea, hold her hand and do anything they could to ease the pain in the weeks that followed. Once again, the house was constantly filled with every kind of cake, sandwich, stew and soup under the sun. Those around Bridie knew they couldn't fix her heart, but they were determined that her stomach would never be empty!

This was a terrible season in Bridie's life, yet her trademark tenacity and positive nature meant that, despite her tears, she was able to conquer the grief, even if it had a habit of returning on a daily basis. In the midst of all the surrounding noise and chatter, Bridie was still able to hear the whispers of her soulmate. She yearned to see his smile and his beautiful blue eyes, to feel his deep love as he spoke to his "wise wee wummin" and to hear the familiar laughter as they giggled together. All of these things had been taken from her with Mick's passing, yet they lived on in her heart and she still cherishes them today. They had truly been a match made in heaven, and that's where the pair will pick up their story when Bridie is called home herself.

In the meantime, life went on. When all her heart wanted to do was break into a million pieces, Bridie somehow found a way to move forward. She was close enough to God to know that he was giving her strength at that time. She had faced the greatest of tragedies in losing her son, but she knew she would have to dig deep again if she was to get through her life without Mick. Bridie was lonely without him, yet she knew she was never alone. She hadn't asked for any of this, yet in the midst of a journey involving many twists and turns she placed her hope firmly in her Saviour and gave her life into his hands. She knew even then that only God could carry her through her grief.

Christina was worried her precious aunt would go under at this time and wished she could make everything better for her. Sadly, there was nothing she could do but be there by her side. The younger woman was once again impressed by her aunt's courage and demeanour. She was ever the lady, even in her grief. Although she would collapse and cry on occasion, she always managed to pick herself up and go on. Christina could see that it was her aunt's strong faith that kept her going.

Jacqueline was also amazed by Bridie's ability to cope in the days and weeks after Mick's passing,. She knew her friend was in an excruciating amount of pain, yet Bridie tried so hard to put on a brave face when she was around other people. Martin felt equally proud. They all knew she was devastated, yet he watched as she dug deep and somehow found a strength to go on. He wasn't surprised that she busied herself with helping others to help deal with her grief.

Six weeks after his death, Bridie saw a piece of footage featuring Mick in Moldova. She saw the familiar cheeky face smiling through the television screen at her, his loving blue eyes encouraging her to dream of one last dance, one last embrace. She wanted to be close to him so badly. But it was the way he was reaching out to the poor and broken on the filthy streets of Moldova that really shone through. There her beloved husband was, opening his arms and heart to those around him. How she longed for those arms to be around her. How she ached to feel his heart beating next to hers. But as she saw afresh the incredible impact he had made and how many people he touched, something stirred inside Bridie; something that would give her purpose as she adjusted to life without her man. The magnitude of who her husband was and what he had achieved suddenly hit her.

However, while it was clear what she should be doing, she wasn't sure how to go about it. Bridie without Mick seemed like bacon without eggs or fish without chips, but she discovered that new recipes were being prepared. She learned that those who offer themselves to the Lord find that he graciously accepts this offer and couples it with opportunity. Bridie soon realised she would need plenty of patience and a passport for all that lay ahead! Mick McGoldrick had left the earth, but his huge heart and mission to love everyone in Jesus' name had come to rest on Bridie. She could almost see his smile as he encouraged her from paradise: "Come on, ya wise wee wummin. Listen to God." So that's exactly what she did.

CHAPTER 20:
Charity Begins At Home...
And Away

A new chapter was about to begin for Bridie, but she still wasn't sure exactly what it would entail. It wasn't long before she found out. The couple's faithful friend and Mick's constant companion in Moldova, Tom Lennon, came to see her, and he had a plan. God didn't simply take Bridie's pain away, but he gave her the grace to cope and a way to handle it. The way he made for Bridie was to get her more involved in the charity.

Tom asked her to become a director, which would see her take over some of the responsibilities Mick had taken on. Bridie was hesitant at first, doubting whether she could do the job given that she had no idea what was required. Yet every time she thought of the poor, starving people in Moldova she knew there could only be one answer. All along she had been learning from Mick without even knowing it, and the Holy Spirit had taken her on an incredible journey. Tom and all the other volunteers were ecstatic when Bridie agreed to come on board. The work that had begun with Mick at the helm would soon continue, even if things were likely to move a little more slowly due to her inexperience.

Bridie prayed about what she should put her hand to first. There was no way she could ever replace Mick, but there were certainly things she could do to help. She felt guided to keep things simple, so she decided to tackle some of the charity's paperwork and bookkeeping records. The first time she got the laptop down Bridie just sat looking at it with a bank statement in her hand, unsure how to use the software. But then she did what had always worked for her in the past and cried out: "Please help me, Lord!"

It took her eleven hours to work out how to put that one bank statement on the system, as she had absolutely no clue what she was doing and made several mistakes along the way. But she finally did it, and the next time she got it down to ten. It eventually took her just two hours to put up all the remaining statements. Bridie attributes this success to God, as she still felt as though she had no idea what she was doing!

Tom was truly relieved that the charity was able to continue despite Mick's absence. The work they had begun was incredibly important to so many, and the people of Moldova still badly needed their assistance. The Moldovans were also reeling from Mr Mick's unexpected death. He was more than just a nice man who brought them provisions; he had also been their friend. He had showed them an unconditional love that had touched their hearts deeply.

Tom visited one old lady who said that she had suffered horrendous loss and hardship under communism and had lost all trust in mankind, but she explained that Mick McGoldrick had shown her how to love again. She said he was special; that he had loved so much and so freely it had unlocked something deep inside her again. Everywhere Tom went he found people mourning but also celebrating the life of his best friend. It was touching and completely fitting for Mick to be remembered so fondly.

Life had started moving at a different pace for Bridie. Hours seemed to last for days, yet the months also seemed to be flying by. She had to adjust to life on her own, yet all her heart wanted was to be with her boys. Surrounded by her friends and family, and drawing on her faith more than ever, she found a way to cope with the loneliness. She was still a regular at her local chapel and at the weekly bingo, which she was helping to run by this point. It had previously been just a few hours of fun, but the bingo had become a project for Bridie, as she organised the prize money, kept the records, got everything set up before it began and worked with other ladies to ensure it all ran smoothly. Life would never be the same, but as the seasons changed Bridie's strength gradually returned, and bit by bit she came to terms with all that had happened to her.

Popular in the community, Bridie is known by many of the local paramilitary leaders. Although Northern Ireland has thankfully enjoyed more peace since the Good Friday Agreement of 1998, there were still many victims of the unrest that had plagued this country for so long. The powder keg situations that had engulfed the community at Drumcree and robbed Michael of his life were fewer and farther between, but there was still division in Northern Ireland, and too many families like the McGoldricks had to pay the ultimate price.

Mick and Bridie learned through Michael's death that nothing goes away if it isn't addressed properly. Following the murder, they made it their life's work to demonstrate the change that can take place through the love and forgiveness of God. It's not easy to stand up against distrust and hatred, but Bridie has always found it worthwhile.

Once again, she got her head down and gritted her teeth. Northern Ireland was her home, and she felt as though she was surrounded by her own people, yet part of her heart was in Eastern Europe. She began to thrive in her role as director, focusing on what she could do to alleviate suffering most effectively. Although the work was a real mission field for Bridie as she endeavoured to reach out to people with the practical love of Christ, it was extremely difficult to keep going at times. She often wanted some sage advice from her beloved, and she generally found it a great struggle to do life without him.

Not only did United Christian Aid survive Mick's death, however; it actually went from strength to strength. Although the people of Moldova had been shocked and grief-stricken by the loss of their precious Mr Mick, they soon realised his wife was just as committed to ensuring that they weren't abandoned. The charity was given new premises in Lurgan, which were large enough to use as a shop. This meant they could sell the goods they were given to raise funds for the people of Moldova.

Word soon spread about the new shop, and the charity was quickly swamped with clothes, furniture, ornaments and books, all of which needed to be displayed, priced and stacked. It was a massive undertaking, but Bridie rose to the challenge, using her Carr's experience to ensure that the shop was tidy, welcoming, well stocked, running in an orderly fashion and giving customers the best opportunity to get what they wanted.

She didn't need to have a broom out the back to do fake repairs this time round, but Bridie soon realised she needed eyes in the back of her head. Not everyone who came into the shop was there to pick up a bargain or to give to those in need. Time and time again she had to stop people shoplifting. She came to know which ones to watch, and it was an amusing sight to see this diminutive woman in her sixties insisting any prospective thieves empty out their bags before she called the police.

Bridie also had endless arguments with people who wanted to haggle over the price of an item. Often they would protest that they had absolutely nothing and couldn't afford the price on the tag. But Bridie would smile sweetly and ask: "Do you have a house to live in? Running water? Clothes on your back? Bread to eat? Right, then you have far more than the people your money will be going to. That's the cost. If you can't afford it, put it back!" It wasn't that she didn't care for the poor in Ireland or those who were struggling with ill health; it was just that the poverty she had seen in Eastern Europe was so severe she knew it was vital they got the help they needed… and paying 50p for a good winter scarf wasn't a big ask!

As well as running the shop and overseeing the volunteers who helped there, she also served as a personal shopper. Often she would find out what customers were looking for, especially if there was a particular occasion they were preparing for. She would set about getting them sorted from head to toe with a lovely outfit including coordinating hat and shoes. Bridie also enjoyed helping poor families in the Lurgan area find bargain furniture so they could make their homes more stylish without spending much. She would take them around the large shop, which had different areas for clothes, furniture, books and so on, and would help them kit out entire rooms.

Bridie was constantly amazed at the generosity of people from all over the country, many of whom donated valuable items in excellent condition. She knew that it was as much to do with her husband's legacy as the plight of the folks in Moldova that prompted people to give. She had several volunteers who would go all around Northern Ireland in the United Christian Aid van collecting the donations. They also helped in the shop, setting everything out, loading items into customers' cars and serving them if it was busy. Three men – Noel McIntyre, Noel McGinn and Terry Lewsley – were with her for several years and proved to be a real blessing as a result of their helpfulness and banter. They kept Bridie on her toes, but she knew they were always looking out for her and their kindness to her over the years was a big help.

They still had to pack up the van for Tom to take goods over as he continued to travel out with some of the volunteers to feed and arrange sponsorship for people in the poorest Moldovan villages. The need for warm clothing, sanitary products, shoes, bed linen, towels, toiletries, and kids' resources never changed. The longer Bridie was with the charity the more she understood how much Mick had done while he was alive, and all without a single complaint. He had just quietly and faithfully served the lost, which made her love and miss him all the more. She had always known, without a doubt, that she had the most amazing husband in the world!

It was a busy, hectic time, but it gave Bridie the one thing she thought she would never have again: hope. Getting up each day with things to do and people to help gave her life purpose, and the long days eventually turned into weeks and then months. Once again, those who knew her best were amazed by her tenacity and willpower, despite her broken heart.

Ever since those early days on the streets of Glasgow, Bridie has loved to laugh, joke and entertain, but her real passion is making sure everyone else is taken care of. She simply cannot stop thinking of ways to assist people. Whether that involves writing to the council for her friends or cooking breakfast for hungry biographers, she is completely unstoppable!

With her hope slowly returning, Bridie settled into a new phase of life she had never wanted or imagined. Alone in their family home, she adorned the walls with more photos of her boys than ever before. Bridie's love for interior design had never left her, so, accompanied by various family members and friends, she redecorated the house in a range of beautiful colours and styles. She wanted to ensure that her home would always remain a place of warmth and welcome with a little wow factor thrown in. She even painted intricate designs onto little ornaments to match her colour scheme. No stone is ever left unturned when Bridie is at work.

Christina was impressed but not surprised that her Aunty Bunty continued to be as tenacious as ever, given that she had always been the strongest person she knew. Although she hated seeing Bridie go through so much heartache, she was inspired by the way her aunt continued to shine for others. Bridie had been there for Christina her whole life, dispensing love, laughter and wisdom, and she wasn't about to step back at this point. She often told her niece that her ears were always there to listen, and Christina has taken full advantage of this on many occasions, knowing that Bridie is easy to talk to and excellent at giving sound advice. Nothing is too much for Bridie when it comes to her family, and the saying "brought together by blood, kept together by love" sums the relationship up well for Christina.

Time stands still for no hard-working man or woman, and the first anniversary of Mick's death came around far too quickly. There was no place Bridie could go to escape it, so she accepted Tom's invitation to go to the very place Mick had spent his last days. Despite her asthma and crippling arthritis, she set off to be in the places and with the people that had captured her beloved Mick's heart.

CHAPTER 21:
Up, Up And Away

A special Mass was held for Mick in every village they visited, and it was so touching for Bridie to see such an outpouring of love for him. One day she and Tom were going into a cathedral when a woman stopped them and introduced her eighteen-year-old son to Bridie. She told her, through a translator, that Mick had sponsored the boy out of his own pocket so he could get an education, and that he was now working and able to support her. The woman said that Mick's name would live on through every generation in the village, and that they prayed for him and for Bridie all the time. Then she took Bridie's hand and said: "You've lost such a wonderful man."

While attending a service at another cathedral to celebrate her husband's life, Bridie sat beaming with pride as the bishop delivered a speech of gratitude for everything Mick had been and all that he had done for them. He said Mr Mick had taught him the true meaning of unconditional love, and that he had wanted to help everyone, with no exceptions. Mick hadn't cared about lice or filth, he had just hugged everyone and given everything he had to help those without the most basic of necessities.

However, Bridie soon found out as she travelled around that their admiration wasn't reserved solely for Mick. One day she was taken through the towns and villages on a horse and cart. Everywhere they went, people came out to say thank you for everything Mick had done and for the work of United Christian Aid. The man who owned the cart was busy talking away to Bridie all the while. She didn't understand a word he was saying, so she simply smiled and nodded in a friendly way. Tom was laughing away to himself, as he was able to speak and understand some of the language. He eventually told her the man had been proposing to her, promising her a wonderful life with him. Bridie was thoroughly embarrassed and asked Tom to tell him thanks but no thanks, but Tom just kept laughing. He pointed out that the man had his own business… what more could she possibly want?

Even a horse and cart couldn't tempt Bridie, however. There had been, and only ever would be, one man in her heart. She politely asked the interpreter to tell everyone who was listening that no one could replace her Mick. Meanwhile, she felt very foolish sitting on the cart with everybody bringing her flowers and shaking her hand, as if she were some kind of celebrity. Just like Mick, Bridie didn't want anyone to put her on a pedestal; she was simply there to love them and to introduce them to Jesus any way she could.

Amusingly for Bridie, people kept saying: "Look at Mr Mick's wife. Doesn't she look like him?" Some people might have considered being compared to a man a little insulting, but Bridie knew what they meant. They could see the same love for them and for Jesus in her that they had seen in Mick. Far from being insulted, she was thrilled to hear this, and of course she hugged everyone just as much as he had.

One place that was too painful for her to visit was the village where Mick had died. It caused Bridie great torment whenever she considered his last hours and the fact she hadn't been with him. Still, she knew Mick had died in the place he had poured so much of his heart and soul into, and she felt strangely comforted when she saw how much he was missed. In the broken, wounded hearts of a people who had lost a man they had come to trust she saw an understanding of her own grief. These people truly loved her husband; not just for what he had done for them, but for who he was.

One village decided to hold an outdoor service rather than in a church, and had set up a table in his honour. Bridie knew these people had nothing, yet they wanted to do something special to remember him. She was the guest of honour, and they treated her like royalty as she sat at the rickety makeshift table they had laid out for her. Many of the people brought out photographs of Mick with their families. In every image he was smiling and surrounded by clambering children. They kept saying: "Mr Mick always gave us a hug. He always made us feel special." Once again, Bridie felt overwhelmed with love for her man and with sadness that he was no longer there.

Mick had been granted a wish that was very dear to his heart during the last year of his life, albeit quite by accident. He had always wanted to spend Christmas Day celebrating the Lord's birth with those who were the poorest and neediest. Mick had often mentioned his desire to be in Moldova for Christmas, but Bridie had been adamant that they should spend Christmas at home with their family. He already gave so much of his time to the poor, and she had wanted Mick home with them at such a special time of year. Mick had gone out to Moldova in the January before his final trip in April. He normally would have gone later in the month, but he went out right at the beginning that year. Sounding absolutely delighted, Mick called Bridie to say that he was so grateful to God as Christmas was celebrated on 6th January in Moldova, so his wish had come true after all! Bridie considered this a real blessing, and was encouraged that the Lord had given Mick one of his heart's desires before calling him home.

Bridie's time in Moldova was incredibly special. Despite being unable to speak the language, she had forged lifelong friendships and made lasting memories. It was soon time to travel home, but she returned to Ireland with increased resolve and passion for the work they were doing. She had a greater desire than ever to help put a smile on a mother's face or to provide food and shelter for one of the impoverished families she had met on her trip.

Just as she had been back in the Gorbals, Bridie was adamant that every human being deserved to have access to all the essentials in life. She had seen at first hand how distrustful a village could be of strangers, but she had also seen that those who went in with the love of God – doing the simplest things, like putting an arm around someone and standing with them in their pain – were able to bring down many barriers.

Back home, Bridie worked as hard as she could to keep the shop stocked and operating. Meanwhile, Tom continued to visit Moldova and, along with various volunteers, drove around Northern Ireland collecting donated clothes and goods. Life was busy for Bridie, and her heart was full of love for the people they were helping.

Although she had a great deal of responsibility with the charity, this was not a good time for Bridie in terms of her health. Her arthritis was badly affecting her movement and her asthma was dangerously debilitating. The whole family was concerned about her, as they could see that working so hard in the shop was taking its toll. There was no way Bridie would agree to stop helping those in need, but everyone was concerned that she was doing too much.

Bridie was usually to be found in her lovely, welcoming home or in the shop selling goods for Moldova. Firm but fair, her volunteers knew she always had the charity's best interests at heart and that they were there to make a difference to some of the most vulnerable people in Europe. Mick had always said that God's love was unconditional and that his charity should be the same way, so Bridie tried to bear this in mind in all her dealings. Another Christian belief that had driven Mick, and continued to drive Bridie, was that of heavenly rewards. He had often laughed at folks who wanted recognition or payment for their charity work, saying: "You'll get your wages and your bonuses a split second after you die!" Another of his favourite phrases was: "We're here to help the needy, not the greedy!"

It was still a real family affair at United Christian Aid, especially when Andrew decided to get involved. He was fifteen years old and becoming a tall, strapping lad like his dad. Andrew had been deeply impacted by the photos and footage he had seen of the work the charity was doing in Moldova, and had been so close to Mick and proud of everything his grandpa had done that he offered to do all the Gift Aid administration. The pair had enjoyed an incredibly strong bond, especially as Andrew had spent so much time with Mick and Bridie during his childhood. It meant so much to Bridie to see her grandson putting all his energy into the charity.

Emma was at university by this point. Bridie was incredibly proud and knew her son would have felt the same way. Emma had always been a studious girl growing up, and much to the delight of her family she earned herself a degree in biomedical science. Sadie continued to impress Bridie with the way she managed to cope with the heartache she had suffered in losing Michael and then Mick. It was wonderful for Bridie to have her loved ones close by, supporting her. After all, family had been so important to Mick.

Mick had often told people to keep coming back to the cross and the love of God; to get their strength from Him. This wise wee wummin knew that was exactly where she needed to be on a daily basis. But while leaning on her love for Jesus gave her the strength to carry on, she was still suffering the loss of her husband terribly, and even when the house was full she often felt alone. She heard so many stories about how wonderful Mick had been and how much he had blessed people, but sometimes they were just too hard to hear. She would be told how he had made someone laugh or helped someone with something, but inside she would be thinking that he was all hers. Her Mick. Her husband. She missed him like crazy every day.

It was Bridie's absolute belief that charity was the Lord's work, and that she was loving people in his name, that drove her on. Nothing could keep this irrepressible woman down, and inspired by how well things were going in Moldova, she embarked on another long trip to visit the poorest of peoples. This time Bridie was drawn to Africa, and her travels took her to the home village of long-time family friend Father Charles in Malawi. She might have been getting older, but Bridie McGoldrick was also growing bolder!

Bridie's friend Moira joined her on the trip and they travelled out to see Father Charles's homeland, visiting two of the villages they were personally sponsoring. Bridie had packed two suitcases filled with items for two young priests who were being ordained, including chalices, Bibles and robes. The cases weighed more than the permitted 60kg but, undaunted, she told the bemused baggage handler she was taking these items to help the poor and should be allowed to do so without having to pay an additional fee. The baggage hander let her take them through without any charge, much to the surprise of Bridie's travelling companion.

It was a gruelling, exhausting trip for the increasingly frail Bridie, but she knew it would all be worth it to see Father Charles and meet his family and friends. He had been shunned when he first left Malawi to become a priest, so it was really special to be there to see him celebrated by his nearest and dearest as he was appointed priest to a local chapel.

Bridie loved the joyful dancing and clapping as everyone praised God and had fun. She and Moira were something of an attraction, as very few white women in their sixties came to visit the village. As the festivities continued, the villagers were all calling Bridie and her friend ugogo, a term of endearment used for a grandmother, which carried with it a sense of honour.

Fun and frolics were never far away when Bridie McGoldrick was in town. In the midst of the celebrations, one man seemed to be dancing right at her. He was really going for it and kept staring at Bridie as he made his dramatic moves. She realised he was challenging her to a dance-off, and naturally she couldn't refuse. Bridie rose up out of her seat, grabbed her crutches and began dancing in response. She was getting down low on her knees, dancing right back at him and making everyone laugh. Shocked and startled, the man ran away! Bridie has always loved entertaining people, but her challenger certainly wasn't expecting this seemingly meek, middle-aged Westerner to respond in kind. Father Charles was splitting his sides laughing because he knew exactly what she was like and had expected nothing less.

One thing Bridie struggled with on mission trips was her need for cleanliness. The jungles of Malawi are not known for their heavy cleaning regimes, and while she was prepared to suffer a little, one little creature guaranteed to make her blood boil was hanging around in droves. Ants! Everywhere she went there were millions of them. As hygiene levels weren't brilliant, the tiny creatures were crawling over everything all the time. Bridie hated them and spent hours scrubbing things in an attempt to keep them at bay. She accidentally discovered that if she halved an orange the ants would disappear, as presumably they didn't like the smell. From that point on she kept an orange with her everywhere she went.

Bridie was delighted to be in Malawi to support Father Charles, but she also took the opportunity to teach the female villagers some basic hygiene methods, especially in the kitchen. She was really keen to communicate the need for cleanliness when preparing food; not in a judgmental way, as the facilities were so basic, but to encourage people to be a bit more careful in order to avoid spreading diseases. Bridie hadn't been prepared for the way people were forced to live there, and once again found the level of poverty they were experiencing absolutely heartbreaking.

The local chief watched her cleaning up everywhere she went and started taking notes. With her usual practical kindness, she encouraged him to use vinegar or hot water to clean. He asked her to teach his wives how to do so. Quick as a flash, she said: "Sure, then you'll have me boiling in the pot afterwards!"

Father Charles gasped and held his breath, waiting on an angry response from the volatile chief, but when the interpreter relayed Bridie's comment the chief just burst out laughing, as he knew she was only playing with him. The African dignitary clearly saw the joker in Bridie as well as a beautiful soul. As ever, Bridie shared common sense along with charity and a sense of fun along with practical assistance. This ensured that she was lauded, applauded and followed wherever she went.

Intent on making a lasting, sustainable impact, Bridie and some of the charity's other supporters donated money to obtain a water tank and an oven, which really made life better for the whole community. The villagers got a mill up and running and were able to bake bread for themselves. They also started a co-op and everyone got involved, and from that point on they were no longer dependent on handouts.

Bridie was held in high esteem by the whole community and fondly remembers the day the villagers showed her just how much she meant to them. Bearing in mind they had nothing, she was overwhelmed when they all gathered together and put on a special ceremony. She was truly embarrassed as they sat her at the centre of the massive crowd, perched on a three-legged stool. The main part of the ceremony involved the village presenting her with a live goat. She was extremely moved, as she knew how much a goat meant to those who had nothing. But grateful as she was, Bridie couldn't help picturing herself sitting beside it on the plane on the way home. Even the famous McGoldrick patter would have struggled to get a goat through customs! Father Charles was delighted by the event in many ways, partly because it was the first time he had ever seen Bridie speechless, though it didn't last long! She smiled graciously and showed her thanks to the villagers, then whispered to Father Charles that he was not to kill it until after she had left.

Growing up, Bridie had always known that her dad had been married before, years before he met Christine, and that she had a half-brother, Bernard, known as Barney. He had been killed in service in Southern Rhodesia (now Zimbabwe). Bridie remembers her dad reading aloud a letter Barney had written, which said: "Aw, Daddy, I wish you could see this. I'm standing beneath the Southern Cross and it's so beautiful." Bridie had intended to visit the spot he had written about while she was in Malawi but was sadly unable to because of unrest in the area at the time.

One night as she was coming back from a sightseeing visit to the capital city, Lilongwe, Bridie was desperate for the bathroom. Father Charles and the friends they were travelling with stopped to let her go in the bush, but about fifty people suddenly appeared, so she had to get back in the car and they drove on. They went a little way up a mountain, and as she was so desperate by this time she got out and went by the roadside.

Just before she got back in the car, Bridie looked up and noticed that the sky looked absolutely beautiful. The stars were so stunning it took her breath away. She was mesmerised and felt a deep, unexplainable feeling stir within her. She was rooted to the spot and felt incredibly emotional for some reason. The constellations above her head seemed to be calling her name, and something in her soul was deeply touched. She encouraged her friends to come out and take a look, but they were too tired. Eventually, Father Charles came out and looked up. Then he said: "Ah, Bridie, do you know what that is? It's the Southern Cross."

Bridie felt so blessed and grateful to have seen it. She had been unable to get to her brother's war grave, yet there she was looking up at the very stars he had written about in that letter all those years ago. Bridie has no doubt God had ordained that moment for her, and it felt truly amazing. She just wanted to reach up and touch the stars, and she truly saw the glory of God in all that beauty. It still takes her breath away whenever she pictures the stars on the inky black sky that night, and she is so thankful for that beautiful, majestic moment, which felt so tender and personal.

Bridie reluctantly left Malawi after an exhausting but hugely blessed trip, having experienced the highs and lows of life for some of the world's poorest, most joy-filled people. Goats aside, Bridie took a great deal home from her trip, and Malawi will always hold a special place in her heart.

CHAPTER 22:
Still Running The Race

Back home, Bridie continued to immerse herself in the work of the charity and in serving her local community. Her friend Alice, who lived two doors along, was a constant companion on her trips into town, and on one occasion Bridie decided to put a smile on the shopping centre manager's face. She approached him and said she wanted to lodge a complaint against him. He was really taken aback and flustered, and immediately started apologising.

When he asked what she wanted to complain about, Bridie, completely straight-faced, said that she and her friend had been going there for months and passed him every time, yet he had never once stopped or searched them, which was a great source of disappointment to her. The poor guy was shocked at first, then looked up at the two older ladies and burst out laughing. He said she had brightened up his day and that he would look out for them every time they came in from that day on. This amused Bridie, not just because it was a "wee laugh", but because it gave her great joy to make people smile and enjoy the moment. Alice laughed all the way round the shops that afternoon!

In the same shopping centre on another occasion Bridie ended up inside a snow globe. It had been set up for children to have their picture taken with Santa, but Bridie announced she was going in. Alice was horrified at the thought of clambering into a giant plastic bubble for everyone to see, but as she had never had her picture taken with Santa, even as a child, she agreed to follow her friend in. Santa was rather surprised to see the two old ladies crawling in beside him but had a good laugh about it and happily posed for photos with them. Bridie threw an arm around him and they smiled away as a crowd of people gathered around, laughing. It wasn't until they were getting out that Santa said: "Well, that was the first time I've ever had my butt felt in a photo!"

Given how small she was and how tall Santa was, and having sunk down into the snow globe, Bridie realised that while she had thought she was innocently holding on to the back of his padded waist, she'd actually had her hands on his backside the whole time. She felt so embarrassed! She still laughs about it today, and the photographs continue to make an appearance every Christmas.

Another ritual she has faithfully observed for many years is cooking tea for Alice and running it over to her house before eating her own. A grateful Alice, now in her late eighties, waits with eager anticipation, especially the nights Bridie's legendary chips and chicken curry are on offer.

Superhuman though her efforts may have been, she was but one woman, and her health had begun to slow her down quite considerably. Her family continued to support her, but Bridie's medical issues prevented her from doing some of the things she had done previously. Walking had become extremely painful, and on one occasion it literally got her down. She was on the top step of a ladder one night doing some painting in her house, trying to ignore the pain and effort this required. She was exhausted, so she came down from the ladder and had a shower, then prayed: "Lord, I'm so tired and sore. I could really do with a break."

Her prayer was quickly answered, though perhaps not in the way she had expected. Bridie was in the charity shop the next day when she completely missed a step and fell to the ground. She was in agony and couldn't move her left leg. She called out to her two volunteers for help, and they fetched Sadie, who took Bridie to hospital. She had her leg X-rayed and was told she had a bad sprain, which would be fine after a few days' rest.

Several days went by, but Bridie definitely wasn't fine. The pain had intensified, in fact. She was in constant agony and none of the pain relief was helping. Bridie was so grateful Sadie was a nurse and was there to help her, as she couldn't even make it to the bathroom on her own. Sadie was adamant it was more than a sprain and insisted she be taken back to hospital, despite Bridie's protests. The same consultant she had seen the first time around was still convinced it was nothing serious, but they kept Bridie in as she had developed cellulitis and the doctors were concerned it could lead to septicaemia if left untreated.

As a result of Sadie's persistence and Bridie's exasperation, she was sent for an MRI. It turned out she had broken the top of her foot in two places and had a very serious fracture in her heel. It was no wonder the painkillers hadn't been working! Bridie was extremely dismayed when the medical staff suggested she would be kept in for six to eight weeks, exclaiming loudly that she wouldn't be staying in for six to eight minutes!

An orthopaedic consultant had become involved by this point and was very concerned about the condition of her foot. Bridie was reluctantly admitted and forced to endure complete bed rest. Unsurprisingly, she was surrounded by friends and family, and she soon had the hospital staff entertained as well. She liked to talk to everyone, sharing stories and trying to amuse those around her.

She quickly observed that most of the doctors and nurses worked incredibly hard and were under intense pressure to get everything done without enough staff on hand. She was immensely grateful to those who did their best and looked after her well. Some, however, were less helpful. One time she pressed the bell to call a nurse as she needed the toilet and couldn't get there herself. The nurse told Bridie to wait a minute, then left her there, desperate to go, for more than an hour.

For a woman who has always prided herself on dignity and cleanliness, Bridie couldn't put up with being left alone to wet the bed. She was completely disgusted by the lack of care this particular staff member had shown. She said her piece and demanded to be discharged, and her voice was eventually heard. She was given specific instructions to rest and not to stand on her foot, but she was finally allowed to go home.

The nursing care she received in her own little palace was first class, and she couldn't have been treated any better than she was with Sadie, Emma, Andrew, Jaqueline and various other family members and friends looking after her. Sadie was a complete godsend with her practical expertise and her never-ending willingness to help Bridie. She was there all day, washing, ironing and making dinner. They all learned how to help her, and Bridie found a way to wash and dry herself lying down when she was unable to sit up because of her arthritis. She was a happy bunny at home and definitely fared better there than she had at the hospital. Her recovery seemed to go much more smoothly and quickly with the love and warmth of her family and friends surrounding her.

A new chapter in Bridie's life began in which balance, walking, posture, strength and ability were all compromised. More than a decade has passed since that accident, and the large plaster boot she was given to protect her foot is still a permanent fixture. Sadly, nerve damage set in, and the extreme pain she initially suffered increased. The pain often stops her getting up out of her chair or upstairs to her bedroom, so she sometimes has to sleep on the couch downstairs. However, she is as determined as ever not to be a burden to her ever-loving family.

For a while Bridie used a walker to ensure she could get back to the shop and sort out the stock, but the pain was too intense and moving about the premises had become nigh on impossible. As ever, her attitude was a mixture of defiance and compassion. She knew that being in pain wasn't going to feed the poor and was determined to ensure that the work carried on regardless. It was sheer agony, but Bridie did all she could to stay at the helm. The charity was still shipping out clothes and goods as well as sponsoring families and villages, and Bridie kept thinking about the mothers who had nothing to give their children.

Sadly, her health deteriorated further, and she began to suffer from pneumonia on a regular basis. This badly impeded the stubborn Scottish firebrand's progress, finally forcing her to slow down. She was still having terrible trouble with her arthritis and asthma. One minute she would be fine, then she would suddenly collapse and even fall unconscious, often resulting in her being rushed into hospital. It was really scary and the whole family was extremely concerned for her.

Jacqueline actually thought Bridie was going to die on a couple of occasions. The younger woman would sit by the besides for hours just watching the older woman and hoping she would pull through. Bridie bounced back each time, and soon had the nurses and doctors in hysterics at her stories. Jacqueline could hardly believe she was looking at the same person once Bridie had turned a corner.

Martin was also alarmed many times as his beloved Aunty Bridie battled one health setback after another. On a few occasions he was utterly shocked to see her looking so ill lying in a hospital bed. Watching her wince in pain or struggle with her breathing distressed him, and he hated to see her so helpless. Bridie had always been there for Martin and his family, first with their Uncle Mick and then on her own, and he was committed to always being there for the woman who meant the world to him.

Likewise, Christina admitted to feeling a deep concern for Bridie's health, though she no longer expects her energetic aunt to slow down. Despite her constant struggle, Bridie has never taken her health into consideration. She simply puts on a brave face and kept going, always putting others first.

Touched as she was by the unwavering love and support she received from her extended family, Bridie was never happier than when she had a houseful of people to feed and entertain. Life was certainly slowing up, however, and her failing health meant introducing some changes she was very reluctant to make. Gamely, or perhaps stubbornly, Bridie had tried to keep the charity work going, but as she became increasingly fragile the volunteers knew she shouldn't – or even couldn't – continue.

She was still struggling around the shop, barely able to breathe as she tried to serve customers or sort out the stock. One time she collapsed and was rushed back into hospital, where she found herself saying: "Look, if I'm going to die, I'm going to die. What does it matter?" But when she sat back and considered what this was doing to her friends and family she knew that it was time to stop.

So with a heavy heart, and after many discussions with Tom, who was also slowing down a bit, Bridie closed the charity down in 2017. The sponsorship side continued but the trips around Northern Ireland and over to Moldova came to an end, and the shop shut. Although completely unfounded, Bridie felt as though she was giving up on her boys. After all, she had done the charity work for them as well as for the poor. She also felt as though she was letting the people of Moldova down. She still desperately wanted to help, but it just wasn't possible any more. It broke Bridie's heart to shut down, but ultimately she knew it couldn't be helped and that it was the right thing to do. United Christian Aid may not have been sending out provisions any more, but Bridie continued to pray for every family they had met over the years, knowing that Mick would have wanted her to keep them in her heart, just as he had.

It wasn't clear what the future would hold for this wise wee wummin who had crossed over the Irish Sea from the Gorbals to forge a new life in the shadow of Belfast's troubled streets. She has endured more than most will ever have to in ten lifetimes, yet she has always retained her sense of humour, her iron will and her handy stubborn streak. Neither has she lost her sense of wonder at the way her life has turned out, or how God has used her to reach so many different people. She insists that she serves a God who is full of surprises, and her advice to anyone who hears him calling them to something they don't feel qualified for is to say yes, but then to lean on him fully because it will be impossible to do it without him and his grace.

This grace has been evident throughout her life, even before she realised it. As far back as childhood she leaned on the power and providence of God, yet it took the greatest tragedy of her life to fully understand how loving he was. While she has never believed that Michael's murder was God's plan, she is convinced Jesus was there with him that night, holding his hand as he was killed. She also believes Jesus was with the murderer, asking him not to do it. After all, she insists that we all have the chance to respond to Jesus, and that he is a God of love.

God had made himself so known and clear to Mick and Bridie when they were ready to commit suicide, and had given them a new purpose. Even today, Bridie can hardly believe they were able to carry on; not just to exist and get by, but to grow stronger and to learn how to live and laugh again. And laugh she certainly has! No one entering Bridie's home ever leaves without having a giggle or two, usually at some story or other she has regaled them with in her usual animated fashion.

Jacqueline has been amazed by her friend's strength and capacity for fun. Despite the enormous pain Bridie she has experienced, they always had a laugh on their frequent days out. One of Jacqueline's favourite memories is of a day when Bridie and Margaret were haggling with a store manager over garden ornaments. The poor guy didn't stand a chance as the pair had an answer for everything. They were so convincing, and needless to say they got what they wanted. Unfortunately, they had secured themselves so many bargains they wouldn't all fit in the car! Everyone was in stitches at the banter from the pair of them.

Shopping with Bridie is always an amazing experience. She hunts for bargains everywhere she goes, yet she constantly replenishes her well-stocked fridge and cupboards with the food her friends and family love best. If someone happens to mention their favourite chocolate bar it will quickly be purchased by the handful.

Bridie's health concerns have worsened in recent years, and she is now in excruciating pain due to the fusion of her vertebrae and hip, which has made walking, sitting, standing and any sort of movement a trial. Although she can't get up her stairs unless she crawls sometimes, she refuses to give up. Whatever happens, she knows God will see her through. After all, she's fairly sure the Almighty wouldn't fancy having to put up with an irate Bridie for all eternity!

For Martin there is even more reason to be round at Bridie's house these days than ever before, as he has his own kids now and they love her as much as he does. They come in and head straight for her sweetie jar, just as Martin and his brothers had all those years ago. In fact, Martin still heads for the bottomless sweetie jar himself!

The life of Bridie McGoldrick has never been dull or quiet, and it never will be. Her loud, infectious laugh is still as welcoming as ever and her storytelling knows no bounds. Christina considers her aunt to be one of the greatest people in the world and cannot begin to describe how much she loves her. There are few people in life who can be trusted completely, but Christina trusts her aunt with all her heart and has received nothing but love and understanding from her. The queen of cuddles, Bridie has always been full of stories and surprises. And despite fighting a constant battle after losing Michael, Mick and her physical health, Bridie's great faith and love for others has always astounded her niece. Now a mother and grandmother herself, Christina realises even more acutely the agony her aunt has faced over the years and beams with pride when she considers Bridie's strength and resilience in the face of adversity.

Bridie still lives in the beloved Craigavon home she shared with Mick and continues to walk out her faith with the community at her chapel. The ache in her heart for her beloved boys never goes away, but she holds tight to their memories and to the belief that she will see them again one fine day. In her heart, Mick is just as he was that last day she saw him, while Michael is still thirty-one.

Football had always been a popular sport in the McGoldrick family, and Andrew shares his father's love for Glasgow team Celtic. One of the most treasured pictures in Bridie's bedroom is a picture of Andrew wearing his Celtic scarf and standing with Neil Lennon, a Lurgan man who was Celtic manager at the time. Every time Mick and Andrew practised scoring goals Andrew had won, yet fittingly the last Saturday Mick was alive he had won. It was lovely for Bridie to think back to that last day the pair had spent together, given that his grandson was so precious to him. But Bridie doesn't believe the beautiful game is reserved for life on earth alone. Having played it with his son, grandson and many other children, she believes Mick will still be playing football in heaven.

As Bridie considers the life she has left ahead of her, there is no hint of taking it any easier for this dynamic five-foot-one-inch powerhouse. She insists that if God in his wisdom decides to restore her body and health she won't just sit around on her butt. She is excited to think that she might one day be able to get out there and do more to help other people.

Few will travel to the darkest depths of human suffering Bridie has had to go to, and fewer still could emerge as loving, forgiving, generous and compassionate. Whether she finds herself in the poverty-stricken villages of Malawi, Romania or Moldova, or mixing with the great and not-so-great on the troubled streets of Northern Ireland, no one who meets Bridie McGoldrick can deny her faith or her fortitude. She has loved but never lost, for the ones who are now in heaven are cherished forever in her heart. Bridie is a shining example of strength and single-mindedness, combined with a selflessness and a servant heart that she wears beautifully on her perfectly styled sleeve.

Michael often asked his mum in jest, and usually when he was ready for a cuddle, "Sure, I'm a nice guy, amn't I, Mum?" If Bridie were to ask the same question of her nearest and dearest, the answer would be a resounding yes. This wise wee wummin's life has been hugely inspirational to many, as well as fun and entertaining. To be around Bridie McGoldrick is to be around love. As she reflects on her time on earth, all the way from the Gorbals to County Armagh, she feels confident that she has run the race set before her well and made sure her heavenly Father has been made known through the grace he has given her to forgive.

She also knows that when her time on earth is done she will embrace her boys again with all the love she possesses. Then no doubt she'll start bartering with the angels over heavenly furniture, draping colourful curtains over the pearly gates, cooking St Peter the best chips he has ever tasted and topping up heaven's eternal sweetie jars.

Epilogue

Writing this book has been a real labour of love for me. I first met Bridie and Mick in 2005 when I interviewed them for a documentary I was making about healing, and their story of forgiveness touched me deeply. The tears fell freely as I sat listening to this extraordinary ordinary couple share about their lives and the loss of Michael, and I felt they were the most remarkable people I had ever met.

Whenever I watch the news footage or just consider his words, Mick's speech at Michael's funeral inspires and humbles me in equal measure. I knew him only briefly, yet the love and adoration he had for his only child was immense, which makes the power of forgiving those who killed Michael and robbed him of his boy all the more amazing. The grace he showed the killers is completely heroic, and I am in awe of his faith. I still get goosebumps when I think of Mick's heartfelt cry in asking for the fighting to stop. I am also deeply moved by his considered response to the police officer that the worst possible news would be to hear that his son had killed someone rather than be killed himself.

I was truly inspired by the work the couple did for United Christian Aid, and had the privilege of driving around County Armagh with Mick collecting goods for Moldova. What an experience that was, as he was adored everywhere we went. There was a real sense of godliness about Mick; not in an off-putting, holier-than-thou way, but just in the humble way he spoke to people and made them feel as though they mattered. And they really did matter to him. What he went through when he lost Michael was horrific, yet he emerged as this amazingly kind man who simply wanted to love everyone he met.

Another thing that struck me about Mick was how wise he was. A lot quieter than Bridie (most folk are!) he always spoke with a quiet conviction and plenty of common sense. He never failed to listen to people and always sought to bring them gentleness, unity and respect. I was also mesmerised by his eyes, though not in the weak-at-the-knees romantic way his wife is. As I looked into Mick McGoldrick's eyes I could clearly see the love of Christ. That may sound farfetched or even a little crazy, but there is no other way to describe how I felt when I spoke with him.

One big regret in my life is that I never got to travel to Moldova with Mick and Tom to film the work they were doing there. The last time I was with him we agreed that I would go out on the first trip they took after a documentary he and Bridie had taken part in aired, believing it might raise some support for the charity and fund my trip. I was very excited at the prospect as I knew United Christian Aid was doing an amazing work.

Mick told me to watch out for this documentary, which would be shown at Eastertime. I watched it excitedly one Sunday evening, and it was a very interesting programme documenting how Julie Nicholson, an English vicar, had stepped down from her position as parish priest because she was struggling to forgive the killers of her daughter Jenny, who had been just twenty-four when she died in the terrible London bomb attacks of July 2005. She was an extremely honest and brave lady, and I was fascinated by her story.

Riveted, I felt extremely proud when the time came for Mick and Bridie to speak. As ever, their words were laced with grace and compassion. However, to my absolute horror, a photograph of Mick appeared on the screen, and the accompanying words stated that Bridie would need all her strength now as Mick had died in Moldova since the documentary had been made. I was completely stunned! I couldn't believe this terrible news, so I called Bridie. Margaret spoke with me, confirming the worst and informing me that the funeral was just about to take place. I wasn't a family member or even a close friend then, and I hadn't known Mick for long at all, but the loss was palpable and my heart broke for Bridie. It just seemed so unfair.

I was also struck by the enormity of the shock they must have felt all those years earlier on finding out, via the television, that their beloved son had been murdered. I felt as though I had been hit by a brick when I found out this way about Mick, whom I didn't know all that well, so I can't even begin to imagine how it had felt to learn of their only child's death on the television.

At that point I was merely a Scottish lassie who had come over to film them for a TV documentary. Although they had hugely impacted my life I wasn't really part of their lives, but that has certainly changed over the last decade. Since then I have spent many hours in their lovely Craigavon home, surrounded by precious photographs and memories. I can honestly say that, despite all the heartache on display, Bridie's house is wonderfully vibrant. There are always people popping in to visit her, phone calls designed to put the world to rights and delicious food to be eaten.

Bridie is at her happiest when she is looking after people, and I would have considered it very rude to refuse any of her wonderful meals. I can also honestly say that Bridie McGoldrick's chips are about the finest I have ever tasted. Fat, brown, crispy on the outside and fluffy on the inside, they leave a taste of childhood as well as sheer pleasure in your mouth. I have stood over her as she made them, and yes, she boils them first, yes the fryer is up high, and yes the potatoes sit in water for hours before they're fried, but that's it… no great mystery. Yet somehow these chips taste like a little bit of heaven, albeit with a plethora of calories to boot!

For me, spending time with Bridie has gone far beyond the remit of writing this book. She is a friend, and I love doing life with her when I go to visit. She has even got me into watching Korean detective shows with her, although I only ever do that in Craigavon!

Shopping with Bridie is especially fun. I can still see the look of resignation on one store manager's face as he realised he would never beat this human dynamo as she bartered with him over a table, four chairs and a parasol that had been wrongly priced. While the mistake may have been unintentional, Bridie McGoldrick knew her rights and was adamant she should pay the price that was stated on the display, not the extra he was insisting on.

A war of attrition ensued with neither backing down. I could have sold popcorn as a crowd gathered to listen. Bridie was never nasty or overbearing –she was making the poor guy laugh as they debated back and forth – but eventually her tenacity and cheeky smile won and he simply folded. She wasn't smug or arrogant about it either; in fact, she asked after his family and promised to tell everyone to come to the store as he was a decent, fair manager who had his customers' best interests at heart.

We subsequently enjoyed a lovely afternoon in the sun, seated round the new purchase after the store manager had arranged for it to be delivered to her house, free of charge. The experienced confirmed to me that those who take this wee woman on in a battle of words had better be prepared for the long haul!

Friends and family members all speak of Bridie's great strength and tenacity as well as her infectious sense of humour. Over the years I have known her and met her loved ones, everyone has said the same thing: that she is an incredible woman full of love and laughter… and totally unstoppable!

People say you should never meet your heroes or you will be disappointed, and I dare say this is true for some. When I met Bridie McGoldrick I didn't know her name or her story, so I didn't really have any preconceptions. However, over the years of getting to know and love her she has become one of my heroes. She has endured the most profound heartbreak imaginable, in the most brutal circumstances and for the most inexcusable reasons, yet still she chooses to forgive. Then she lost the love of her life, soulmate and best friend, yet still she chooses joy and hope.

The faith she has in her heavenly Father, her saviour Jesus and the Holy Spirit is real and unquestionable. Frailer and less able to move around freely these days, this feisty warrior still warms my heart with her stories and captivates me with her presence. I thank God that he brought her into my life and that she let me tell you her story. Bridie McGoldrick is a dear sister in Christ and a woman of astounding faith. She is also the best chip-maker, sweet supplier, storyteller and wise wee wummin in the world!

About The Author

Lorna Farrell is a natural storyteller; not only through this book, but also through her poetry, speaking engagements, songwriting and stand-up comedy.

One of the songs she co-wrote, *Prize Worth Fighting For* was even a top-ten hit on the Billboard charts!

A former sports broadcaster and TV presenter, she is a regular contributor to BBC Scotland and is currently writing a screenplay based on A Mother's Love. In addition to serving as sports chaplain at Queens Park Women's Football Club, she is an activist against mesh implants, which have left her disabled and in chronic pain.

Lorna is passionate about her Christian faith, dark chocolate with sea salt and colourful footwear. She lives in her beloved Scotland and is a happy mum and mother-in-love, and recently became a gran. She excels at giggling loudly at inappropriate times.

For more info, visit **lornafarrell.com**